Lumumba

Lumumba

Africa's Lost Leader

Leo Zeilig

HAUS PUBLISHING • LONDON

First published in Great Britain in 2008 by
Haus Publishing Limited
26 Cadogan Court
Draycott Avenue
London SW3 3BX

www.hauspublishing.co.uk

This revised and updated edition published in 2015

A CIP catalogue record for this book is available from the British Library

ISBN 978-1-908323-94-1

Typeset in Garamond 3 by MacGuru Ltd
info@macguru.org.uk

Printed in China by 1010

Contents

Léopold's Congo

Later his wife would complain that his hair had been untidy and that there was no question she could attend the Independence Day ceremony with him in such a state. So Pauline Opango did not see her husband deliver the most important speech of his life. He had not been due to speak and there was some surprise in the audience when Joseph Kasongo, President of the Senate, announced the Prime Minister Patrice Lumumba. He moved towards the platform, flashbulbs firing around him. Perhaps Pauline listened to the speech on the radio at home.

> *We are proud of this struggle, of tears, of fire, and of blood, to the depths of our being, for it was a noble and just struggle, and indispensable to put an end to the humiliating slavery which was imposed upon us by force. This was our fate for eighty years of a colonial regime; our wounds are too fresh and too painful still for us to drive them from our memory. We have known harassing work, exacted in exchange for salaries which did not permit us to eat enough to drive away hunger, or to clothe ourselves, or to house ourselves decently, or to raise our children as creatures dear to us. We have seen our lands seized in the name of allegedly legal laws which in fact recognized only that might is right. The Republic of the Congo has been proclaimed, and our country is now in the hands of its own children.*[1]

Henry Morton Stanley was a well established journalist when he began his epic journey across Africa from Zanzibar to the mouth of the Congo River between 1874 and 1877

The Congolese who were present detected no exaggeration in the speech. But the old colonial masters exploded in convulsions of rage at the sight of a Congolese man daring to speak this truth in front of the Belgian establishment. Belgium had occupied the Congo eight decades before in the name of civilisation. Colonial power in the early decades had been absolute and tyrannical.

The King and the Congo

Belgian interest in the Congo was stimulated by Henry Morton Stanley. In 1869, the owner of the *New York Herald* employed the 28-year-old reporter to search for the missionary and adventurer David Livingstone, who was presumed lost somewhere in the Congo. Over a period of 20 years, Stanley more than anyone helped to establish the Belgian empire in the Congo.

Stanley saw enormous opportunities in the Congo for profit. In the welcome he received from the Congolese he imagined great riches: 'In every cordial-faced aborigine whom I meet I see a promise of assistance to me in the redemption of himself from the state of unproductiveness in which he at present lives. I look upon him with much of the same regard that an agriculturalist views his strong-limbed child; he is a future recruit to the ranks of soldier-labourers. The Congo basin, could I have but enough of his class, would become a vast productive garden.'[2]

Stanley came from a poor family. One of many illegitimate children, he entered the workhouse aged six. By 18 he was in America, and he served on both sides of the American Civil War. Promoting himself to journalist in 1867, he reported on India. He was sent the following year by the *New York Herald* to write on a British war with Abyssinia. Ingeniously Stanley bribed the clerks in Suez, to send only his articles back to the United States. A posting as a casual reporter had been transformed into a permanent career.

Perhaps the best way to understand Stanley is to see him simply as a 'speculator'. His books describing his exploration of central

Africa were accounts of the riches that could be found in the region, that were used to entice western states. Stanley systematically detailed the precious woods, ivory and minerals: 'It may be presumed that there are about 200,000 elephants in about 15,000 herds in the Congo basin, each carrying, let us say, on an average 50 lbs. weight of ivory in his head, which would represent, when collected and sold in Europe, £5,000,000.' [3]

The Congo River that Stanley originally sought to map was presented as the principle passage that could be used to access the resources he had painstakingly catalogued. Originally his efforts were directed towards the British, appealing to their seemingly insatiable appetite for African territory. But the British rejected his offers. Stanley then turned to Léopold II, King of the Belgians, who snapped up one of the last regions of the continent as yet unoccupied by other European powers. Stanley met Léopold for the first time in June 1878. By the end of the year he was employed on a contract worth up to 50,000 francs a year (£250,000 in today's money).[4]

Faithful to his new paymaster Stanley was charged with setting up trading stations, and dealing with local chiefs that would ensure Léopold's access to the wealth Stanley had promised. Under the guise of free trade Léopold gave favoured companies concessions to invest in the territory, keeping a majority share for himself. Money flowed almost immediately into Léopold's court.

Stanley persuaded hundreds of Congolese chiefs to hand over sovereignty by signing 'treaties' in the name of Léopold. Adam Hochschild explains what these 'treaties' really were: 'The very word *treaty* is a euphemism, for many chiefs had no idea what they were signing. Few had seen the written word before, and they were being asked to mark their X's to documents in a foreign language and in legalese. The idea of a treaty of friendship between two clans or villages was familiar; the idea of signing over one's land to someone on the other side of the world was inconceivable. Did the

Tales of Stanley's adventures in Africa made gripping reading for British audiences. This illustration on the cover of the *Illustrated London News* relates the history of the canoes being carried up the Inkisi Falls.

chiefs of Ngombi and Mafela, for example, have any idea of what they agreed to on April 1, 1884? In return for "one piece of cloth per month to each of the under-signed chiefs, besides presents of cloth in hand," they promised to "freely of their own accord, for themselves, and their heirs and successors for ever give up to the said Association the sovereignty and all sovereign and governing rights to all their territories … and to assist by labour or otherwise, any works, improvements or expeditions which the said Association shall cause at any time to have carried out in any part of these territories." It was an even worse trade than the Indians made for Manhattan.'[5]

The view that Africa was populated by savages dominated European thought throughout the 19th and much of the 20th century. As late as 1942 a popular geography textbook, *The World: General Geography*, by Dudley Stamp explained to the reader: 'Africa, south of the Sahara Desert, is inhabited almost entirely by negroid peoples with black skins and woolly hair… The opening up of the interior of Africa commenced with the expeditions of explorers such as Livingstone and Stanley. The Negroes were for the most part backward and lazy, as well as being frequently quarrelsome, and so nearly the whole of Africa has come under the rule of European nations. But many groups of negroid peoples are now making rapid progress.'

When Stanley returned to Léopold's court in 1884 he could boast of at least 500 treaties. He also announced that he had founded Vivi, the first capital of Congo and the town of Léopoldville (today's Kinshasa). These were great gifts indeed for the king.

Léopold's fascination with the Congo represented Belgium's position in the world. Belgium was a new state, having only achieved independence in 1830. Across Europe a relatively new class had emerged. The bourgeoisie symbolised the drive for profit and industrialisation, transforming European societies. But in Belgium this class of entrepreneurs and businessmen was less forthright than their European rivals. Ludo de Witte describes Belgium during the period: 'the structure of the Belgian bourgeoisie, which at the time the Congo was created by King Léopold II, was a very young, weak, fragmented class, with little confidence in itself and its projects. It was certainly imperialistic and was trying to organise itself with investments abroad. But the idea of conquering a colony for itself was something that seemed too ambitious for the small bourgeoisie of Belgium. It was only the actions of the Belgian King that ensured the Congo would come into existence and the only way the King could get the Belgian bourgeoisie involved in the "colonial adventure", as it was known, was to give huge concessions to Belgian companies. So what you had was a very small group of very powerful Belgian businesses, who got huge concessions in the Congo, and made super-profits.'[6]

The 1884–5 Berlin Conference attempted to resolve quarrels between European powers scrambling for influence in Africa. The Conference officially recognised Léopold as the legal head of the euphemistically named International African Association of the Congo, soon renamed as the Congo Free State. The stated aims of the new Belgian colony were to abolish slavery – and war would be waged against Arab slave traders for this purpose – and promote free trade.

Cash crops

Initially Léopold gave himself total legal authority in the Congo, which was eventually devolved to an equally despotic system of Governor-General and Vice-Governor. So-called unoccupied land was immediately seized by the state, which meant in practice that white agents could take control of any land they fancied. Originally the enterprise was undertaken in the name of the International African Association, then the International Association. The Association sought to give the private empire a façade of humanitarian concern. Nothing could have been further from the truth.

To fund this humanitarian project require huge sums, so the Association took advantage of the expanding market for rubber and ivory. Land was given to businesses that were then required to farm rubber. These business concessions could operate with impunity in their territory and they were allowed to raise taxes between 6 and 24 francs each year per head of the population. With little actual cash in circulation, the Congolese were expected to produce crops as payment. Massive companies were established. The biggest was the *Union Minière du Haut-Katanga*, established in 1906, which was soon joined by the *Compagnie de Fer du Congo*, and the *Compagnie des Magasins Généraux*.[7]

William Dunlop's invention in 1890 of bicycle tyres made from rubber changed everything. Soon rubber was utilised in many manufacturing processes, in wiring, insulation and vehicular tyres. To meet the demand whole forests were grown for the cultivation of rubber, but in the Congo rubber grew in the wild. There was no need to invest in plantations: the Congolese only had to be forced to cultivate it.

But rubber was not the only cash crop. By 1890 Léopold had quadrupled the export duty on ivory. Within months he announced to his representatives in the Congo that they would benefit from a monopoly on the trade in rubber and ivory. So in 1891 a decree forced the Congolese to provide these goods to Léopold's army of agents. Access to cheap labour was secured through perceived tribal lines. Demands for the new commodities were so great that villages were compelled to hand over able-bodied men for forced labour. When villages were uncooperative, Léopold's new model army – the *Force Publique* – destroyed homes, raped and killed. To prove action had been taken the hands of the victims were removed for payment of bounty.[8]

Resistance and genocide

Evidence of the brutality of Léopold's rule slowly seeped out. By 1906 Alphonse Jacques, a Belgian anti-slavery activist, issued a warning: the entire population of the Congo was threatened with

A closer inspection reveals gruesome details in this early photograph. Native Congolese hold the severed hands of those punished by mutilation for failing to gather enough rubber

'complete extinction'. The combination of famine, forced labour and systematic violence had wiped out millions. According to Adam Hochschild the demographic evidence shows a massive genocide. The population of the region fell from over 20 million people in 1891 to 8.5 million in 1911, recovering slightly in the proceeding decade to reach 10 million by 1924.[9]

But Léopold's victims fought back. There were several important cases of large-scale armed resistance to the Belgians. No sooner than Léopold's regime announced victory in 1894 over the 'Arab' slave traders in the East then further challenges broke out. The official *Encyclopédie du Congo Belge* states that in Patrice Lumumba's home region 'Batetela soldiers were concentrated in Lululabourg. Already angry at being paid late, they then learned that Gongo Lutete, their leader, had been executed by General

Duchesne following an unfortunate error. The Batetela rose and took control of their camp, killing on 4 January 1895 their leader Captain Peltzer. His Lieutenants Lassaux and Cassart, fearing for their lives, fled the encampment. The mutiny became a revolt and soon covered the whole region of Lomami. Officers Gillain, Lothaire and Michaux confronted the rebels, with mixed success.' By October 1896, as many as 5,000 Batetela armed themselves and moved towards Gandu. Eighteen Batetela were imprisoned in April 1900 and quickly executed. However a thousand escaped and hid in the mountains around Lake Kisale, living as guerrilla fighters. The *Encyclopédie* explains that Major Malfey successfully pacified the region in April 1902, but still the rebel fighters remained at large until 1908. Even in this official colonial report there is no disguising the fact that the rebellion lasted 13 years, and secured the brief freedom for thousands of Congolese.[10]

Profits and theft

The official position was that the Congo would be civilised by European rule and that slavery would be crushed. Yet between 1870 and 1960 almost no Congolese had been trained in law, medicine or any higher profession.[11] On the contrary, the exploitation of the population intensified. The Congo had been dragged into an unimaginable state of darkness. But there were clear winners: Léopold's family, the shareowners, banks and businesses. Massive profits were made from the exports which rose in the Congo Free State from 11.5 million francs in 1895 to 47.5 million in 1900 while exports of rubber rose from 580 tons to 3,740 tons over the same period. Just one concession, *Domaine de la Couronne*, earned Léopold 70 million Belgian francs between 1896 and 1905.[12]

King Léopold's Congo Free State was an international concern. Ryan and Guggenheim, the American mining groups, also had interests in the region. But by far the most important business in the mineral-rich region of Katanga was the *Union Minière du*

IN THE RUBBER COILS.

SCENE—*The Congo "Free" State.*

Linley Sambourne's cartoon *In the Rubber Coils* published in *Punch* in 1902 depicts the horrors visited upon the Congolese under the tyranny of Léopold II of Belgium

Haut-Katanga (UMHK). For generations this giant business would dominate the economic and political scene in the Congo. UMHK was essentially a consortium between Belgian and British mining interests, represented by Robert Williams, owner of Tanganyika Concessions Limited (TCL). At one point as much as half of all shares in the business were owned by TCL, which was financed by famous British-based banks such as Barclays, Midland, Barings and Rothschilds.[13]

Evidence of the horrors in the Congo led to a massive international campaign against Léopold's private empire, eventually forcing the Belgian state to 'nationalise' the colony in 1908. The preamble to the deal saw the government pay Léopold the sum of 110 million francs, effectively releasing his control of the Congo and alleviating his 'debt'.

Early years: life in Onalua

When Patrice Lumumba was born on 2 July 1925 the Congo was undergoing rapid change. The initial land-grab and plunder of the Congo was coming to an end. Since the annexation of the Congo by Belgium the colonial state had become more firmly entrenched. The merchants who had operated ruthlessly under King Léopold were by the 1920s recreating themselves as industrialists. In order to support the manufacture of heavy industrial products, the state was obliged to begin spending on schools, hospitals, trains and roads, although the conditions of forced labour in the mines continued, and popular anger against colonialism could not be concealed.

Lumumba was born in the village of Onalua, in the territory of Katako-Kombe in the Kasai province. He was born to the Batetela people. Until 1907 the European presence in the region was fairly limited. Control of the area by the Europeans was achieved only after the execution in 1893 of Ngongo Leteta, an important Arab-Swahili trader who had previously invaded the region. For the villagers the new occupiers were not so different from the Arab-Swahilis: in place of taking slaves the new authority compelled villagers to furnish them with rubber and ivory. The Arab-Swahili slave-trade was replaced with Leopold's own form of slavery.

By 1910 two missions were established in the region. Both missions were set up in competition with each other; one Catholic mission was formed in Tshumbe and another Methodist mission in Wembo-Nyama-Mibango. They soon established schools, run by Catholic missionaries from Flanders and Methodist ones from the United States. Despite the expansion of medical services the region still suffered from a range of serious illnesses. Sleeping sickness, malaria, leprosy and tuberculosis killed hundreds every year. Infant mortality was high.

By 1938 the Catholic mission of Tshumbe included 18 priests, 16 Franciscan nuns, all of them Europeans, 525 male religious instructors and 19 female for a population of 19,944 Catholics and approximately 200,000 'pagans'.[14] The Catholic regime was tightly controlled. After almost three decades of Catholicism in the region, the Batetela still did not have the right to interpret or freely read the Bible.

Missionaries spent their time preaching about the evils of Islam, polygamy and 'paganism'. When Bishop Lambuth arrived from the USA to establish a Methodist mission among the Batetela, he considered them hopeless savages. 'We are thankful that the Methodists in America had a vision to take the Gospel among the Batetela, a cannibal tribe'.[15]

For the village of Onalua the experience of colonisation was brutal. Villagers were forced to work for the new masters, leaving home sometimes for weeks to tap rubber in the surrounding forests so they could meet the targets set by the colonial authority. The church missions often directly served the colony, collecting taxes and distributing punishment for non-payment.

Antoine Omatuku remembers that villagers 'often went as far as Bena-Dibele, more than 200km, to collect enough rubber. Often they would remain several weeks in the forest in terrible conditions.' Even when they returned to the village, the whites could judge the quantity insufficient and punishments would be handed out: 'The *mfimbo* (a braided whip) constituted one of regular punishments in the Onalua: men stretched out on the ground, arms and legs bound, were whipped by policeman, they underwent this torture two or three times per day. Some were killed: nostrils

A drawing of traders weighing balls of rubber gathered by Congolese tribesmen

filled with blood, muscles swollen and torn.'[16] This punishment continued until the 1950s when Lumumba condemned it angrily: *Punishment by flogging was more appropriate for Arab slaves; the Arab era has passed away and this degrading form of punishment should now be completely abolished.*[17]

Colonial adminstration

After Léopold was relieved of his private empire in 1908, the administration of the Congo was radically reformed. In 1910 new administrative structures were established which changed the nature of ethnicity in the Congo. Prior to the intrusion of Belgium, ethnicity was relatively fluid, developing its own political forms of organisation which changed according to regional circumstances. But the colonial regime froze these formations into a system of local government that depended on a fixed definition of ethnicity. Where there were no obvious chiefs they were 'found' by the colonial administration. An active process of the invention of traditions took place. Lumumba had a clear idea of the hybrid nature of this colonial authority: *New customs, half European and half Congolese, have risen as a result of contact with the Europeans, and these have been grafted on to purely traditional customs.*[18]

In the context of the Congo these arguments have been most fully developed by the scholar Mahmood Mamdani. The colonial authorities established Native Authorities which were administrations. Each 'indigenous' ethnic group was allocated their own Native Authority. Membership of a Native Authority was absolutely crucial, as rights to land use – the central source of rural income – was granted on the basis of this membership.

In the colonial period these ethnic authorities ensured access to land and proscribed a specific identity. Native Authorities were the only direct relationship most Congolese had with the colonial state. There was, however, a further tier of state authority that existed in the Congo. This was the one that demarcated the centralised urban authority in the capital – as a largely white and therefore racial zone, so 'the non-indigenous belonged to the civic sphere'.[19] Colonial rule saw the separation between a civic-racialised space that bought together those in urban areas as the 'core beneficiaries of colonialism as "white", and ethnicity as an identity that fragmented its core victims into so many "tribes"'.[20] Certain privileged Congolese were deemed sufficiently civilised and could belong to this white civic space. But most 'natives' were merely 'subjects' to be controlled by Native Authorities.

Copper production, which had started in 1909, expanded rapidly, as the demand for the metal grew during the First World War. It was an 'artisanal' process, where the ore closest to the surface was removed by hand: this required a huge supply of cheap labour. Soon copper became the most important export of the Congolese economy.

The statistics express this development clearly: between 1914 and 1918, Union Minière produced 85,000 tonnes of copper, that earned the company 37.5 million francs, and the Belgian government 7.5 million was in taxes. The impressive expansion of copper production had a ripple effect on the wages of Congolese workers. So between 1918 and 1920, wages rose by 78 per cent.[21] Although progress was slow, living conditions improved. There was also a sizable white industrial class, though neither as large nor as organised as those in neighbouring Northern and Southern Rhodesia and South Africa, and most were supervisors and managers, not workers.

By 1936, there were 18,683 whites in the Congo, approximately two-thirds of whom were Belgian. The others came from Europe and America and worked often as missionaries or skilled employees in the expanding industries. In the 22 years to 1958, there were 113,671 non-Africans (88,913 Belgians), and 7,557 missionaries. This was an extraordinary expansion. By 1945 there were 93 African priests in the Congo.[22]

The genocidal consequence of Leopold's system left a bloody demographic hole in the centre of the Congo. By the early 1950s there were barely 14 million people living in the Congo, an incredibly small population considering the vastness of the territory.[23] As the population grew in the period after Leopold, so did the number of Congolese living in urban areas. In the capital Léopoldville the population rose from 25,622 in 1935 to 388,961 in 1958.[24] Stanleyville (today's Kisangani) also expanded rapidly, from 23,000 in 1935 to 185,000 in 1957. The salaries of the white supervisors and managers were comparable to the wages of civil servants in Belgium. But they lived in enormous luxury, in large houses, driving their own cars. By 1958 the average white salary was 33 times greater than the African average.[25]

Lumumba's family

Patrice Lumumba was the son of François Tolenga and Juliana Amatu. They had four sons, Charles Lukulunga Wetshokonda, Isaie Tasumbu Tawosa (who became Patrice Lumumba), Emile Kalema and Louis Onema Olela. Lumumba's father Tolenga was a Catholic born in 1897. In his youth he participated in the construction of the mission in Tshumbe. He was a farmer, but he also played the *lopondo* (drums) and frequently accompanied a group of dancers in the village. Regarded as unruly, he was imprisoned on several occasions. According to witnesses he was a nervous and occasionally violent man, who was known under the nickname *Kahindola* (angry young man).

Juliana Amatu was married young and knew neither her future husband nor his family. After the marriage she spent time at the mission in Tsumbe. Although officially her second son Isaie Tasumbu Tawosa was born on 2 July 1925, the date is not precise. At the time few were literate, and the date of birth was estimated by proximity to an important event or by the size of the child. Before long the child was know as Lumumba, meaning crowd or team. Lumumba's parents did not remain married. They divorced in 1940. Unwilling to tolerate Tolenga's violence any longer, Juliana finally resolved to leave him.

Juliana was an important influence on Lumumba's life and her energy and determination were certainly characteristics shared by her son. Lumumba's only daughter, also named Juliana, gives us a vivid account of her formidable grandmother: 'I adored my grandmother – I carry her name Juliana Amato. When she died she was between 103–105 years old. She had an enormous amount of courage and an extraordinary zest for life. She was always so positive. She loved drinking and smoking, but still hid when she did so because it had been illegal in her day. But she was also quite a stubborn woman. Until the end she refused to speak in Lingala or Swahili, communicating only in Batetela, even with her grandchildren. But for our cousins who were bought up in the Congo they remembered a woman who was quite severe. When they visited her in the village she would say: "Those who don't work, don't eat – but once the work is done we will party". She also married several times. She divorced my grandfather, saying: "well I was very beautiful, and by the time the next day had arrived I was married again." It is true; she was tall, thin, and you could say beautiful. We were her children, not her grandchildren.'[26]

Lumumba's childhood

From an early age Lumumba forged his own path. Before long he chose his own schools, made his own decisions and fought his own battles. As an adolescent he immediately stood out, as a popular and strong character. Friends and family remember him as curious and audacious, confident in his own abilities. Though he dominated his circle of friends, he was fiercely loyal to them. There was no dispute among his friends that he did not enter, sometimes to stir trouble but always in the end to effect a reconciliation. It was this element of his character that earned him the nickname *Nyumba hatshikala l'okanga* (one who always involves himself).

Lumumba was remembered as an expansive boy, throwing himself into dancing and singing: cheeky and confident. He was never afraid to ask a difficult question, raising doubts about the type of knowledge taught at school on the virginity of Mary and concepts such as original sin. Although rarely attending the Sunday services at the village church, he learnt some French. André Tshupa, a close childhood friend, described a certain stubbornness: 'When he took a decision he did not retreat from it … he had an enormous amount of self-confidence. During our childhood in the village, we often fought. I would strike him down two or three times, but he would never admit defeat. He always had to get his own back, before he would agree to make peace.'[27]

One story told by two childhood friends illustrates well his precocious self-confidence. When he was in the fourth year of primary school the colonial agent for the region visited the area of Onalua to monitor the production of cotton and rubber. The agent immediately complained about the quality of the cotton that came from the inhabitants of Onalua. Intimidated by the white official, the villagers offered him chickens and eggs in apology, a practice taught to them by the missionaries. Lumumba was furious. With two friends he secretly organised to 'ambush' the agent. Fearful of the consequences his friends abandoned Lumumba, who confronted the agent alone. When he had finished he told them that the *Osungu* (white man) wanted to see the father of this audacious little boy.

What's in a name?

Lumumba also chose his own name. Friends were in agreement that while he was in the region of Onalua he was known as *Osungu*. *Osungu* was a powerful title, denoting the white man – the missionary or state agent – in a word the coloniser. The white man was respected not simply for the reasons of skin colour, but because this colour had become associated with wealth and social standing. But it was not only a symbol of success, it was also the tag of fear: for the power that white men held and the fear that they inspired. It was after all the *Osungu* who raised taxes, gave the order for the whip and imposed forced labour.

Lumumba's childhood friends seem to have teased him with the name, calling him 'white man in rags'. It was certainly a source of humiliation for Lumumba, but also partly of pride. He was often the star during festivals, especially among the youth of Onalua. So despite Lumumba's own poverty *Osungu* gave him an important status in Onalua. When he finally left the region, he abandoned the name. In the city the word had an entirely different significance. In Stanleyville he also adopted another name, 'Emery', which appears for the first time in 1946.

Schooling

Lumumba had a reputation as a prolific reader. This reputation was one that stuck; he was known in Stanleyville as the *Okanda doka* (the knowledge magician). When he was born schooling was not a priority for many. Parents would often prefer to keep hold of their children for domestic work and when they were old enough for work in the fields. Naturally there was a colonial twist: child labour was needed to ensure payment of annual taxes. Most boys of 12 or 13 spent three or four months per year on the road, selling meat and vegetables, travelling as far as Orientale Province to buy cloth and material. Schooling was a haphazard process; children would go to a local missionary school, learn a few phrases in French, and then leave again.

There were no state or public schools; all schooling was provided by missionaries. For the people living between the Catholic and Methodist missions of Wembo-Nyama and Tshumbe, schooling was first of all about inculcating a rejection of polygamy, 'superstition' and the consumption of alcohol, identified by the missions as the principle sins of the region.

Lumumba's first period of schooling was between 1931–3 with the Catholic mission. This school welcomed children of 7 to 9 years in two classes. In the first instance children learnt with simple games, but also received religious instruction including how to make the sign of the cross and learnt about the fear of a God who detests 'our sins'. Between 1936–7 Lumumba moved to the Methodist school in Wembo-Nyama.

Most of the teachers in the mission schools had been pupils in the same schools. Although French was taught, much of the teaching was given in the local language. Lumumba liked to mix with older students, with whom he discussed ideas and read their course notes. This was partly because of the poor collection of books available in the school library. Lumumba was one of the school's brightest pupils. Joseph Longonya was a teacher in the school and knew Lumumba: 'Many times my colleagues and I were put to the test by Lumumba; he would approach us at the exit of the class or in the village with French words written either on the ground or on a piece of paper. He asked us to help him read or explain these words ... but our Lumumba had a reputation as a tease ... he knew how to catch us out.'[28]

In August 1941 at the end of two terms Lumumba left school and did not return. One reason was the breakdown of his relationship with his teacher Damase Wungu Shungu. According to André Tshupa, this was caused by Lumumba correcting four mistakes in a phrase that Wungu had written on the board. Humilated by his student, Wungu insisted Lumumba be thrown out. He told friends who accompanied him back to Onalua that they were 'leaving the school because the teachers did not know their work'.[29]

The exclusion illustrates a reality of early missionary schooling in the Congo. Mission schools imposed an authoritarian regime on their students. The head of Lumumba's school had a reputation of being brutal, regularly whipping his pupils. Most schools included a hard physical routine as part of daily life. Each day was marked by crushing millet, fetching water, making and carrying bricks as well as building houses and cutting hay in the fields around the school.

Lumumba enrolled in a school for nursing-assistants in Tunda after having walked for a day to get there. Nursing was a new profession that had started to attract the Batetela. But a former teacher learnt of his transfer and sent a warning recommending Lumumba's exclusion. Once again Lumumba hit the road, without having obtained a school certificate in almost ten years of intermittent schooling. His final 'exclusion' marked a turning point.

Lumumba might have been describing himself when he wrote years later: *The little African boy leaves the paternal roof minus any particle of European civilisation (this is not uniformly true) and goes to school where he ... is taught to read, to write and to do arithmetic. By way of education ... his masters teach him ideas, which although sometimes*

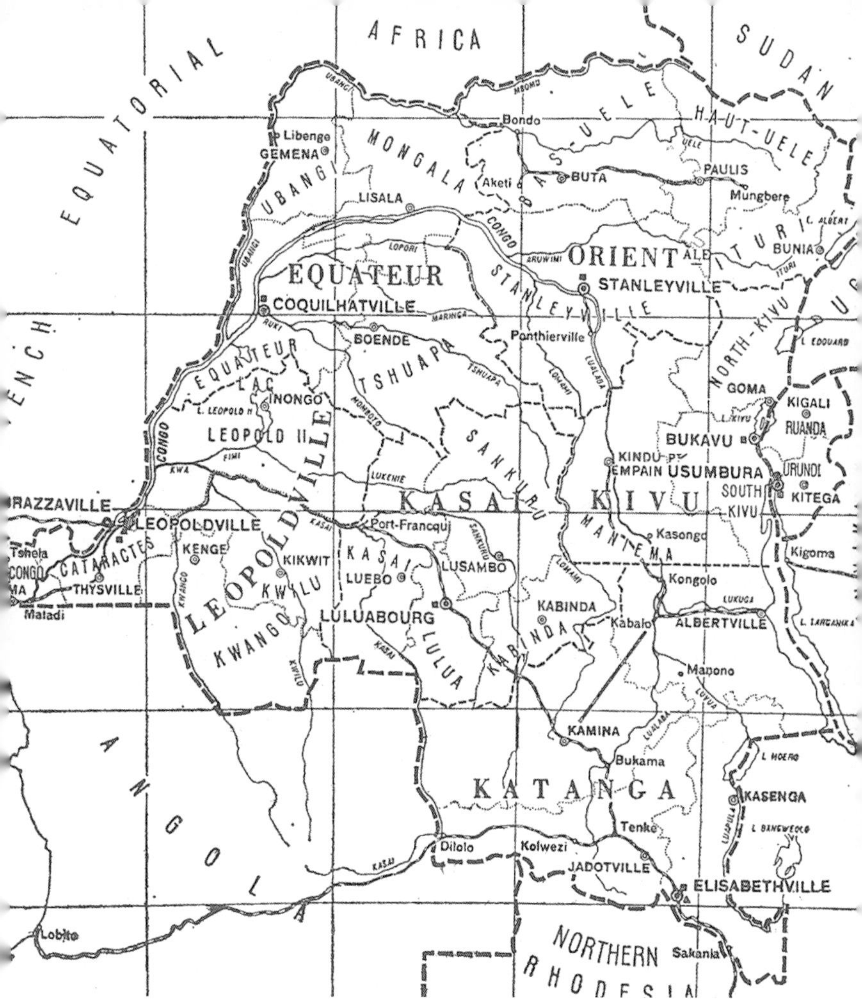

A map of the Belgian Congo in 1958; The names of many towns and cities were changed after the country's independence. A few are listed below:

Léopoldville – Kinshasa
Stanleyville – Kisangani
Elisabethville – Lubumbashi
Luluabourg – Kananga
Coquilhatville – Mbandaka
Jadotville – Likasi
Albertville – Kalemie
Port Franqui – Ilebo

'memorised' take no hold on him, because these ideas have no application in practical life... the black pupil finds himself caught between two conflicting forces: the standards of the school and those of the family.[30]

Towards Stanleyville

When did Lumumba finally leave his region of origin? According to his younger brother, Louis, Lumumba left in 1942. After returning to Onalua from Tunda he stayed only a few hours, arriving at the house in the afternoon and finding his brother he announced that was leaving. He bundled a few things in a bag and left.

Lumumba was not the first to make such a journey. Before 1945 many Batetelas from the region were recruited by different mining agencies, including the *Syndicat Minier Africain* (Symaf) and the UMHK. The UMHK had for a number of years demanded workers from the regional authorities across Kasai. In 1943 the territory of Katako-Kombe saw 12.2 per cent of its male population leave. Alarmed, the authorities of the district of Sankuru forbade the emigration of young men. While the colonial authorities were happy to furnish regional labour to industries – particularly during the 'war effort' – this had to be balanced with the need for labour in the villages. In 1956 Lumumba explained the reasons behind this rural exodus: *to seek work with a view to earning the money they need to get married and enjoy a modicum of comfort (to buy a bicycle, a gramophone, clothing, footwear, etc.) {and} to have a little more freedom than is possible under the yoke of traditional laws and obligations ... the reasons for their exodus are understandable and legitimate; every man has the right to seek to improve his lot by honest means, or to leave his native hearth to seek his fortune elsewhere if he cannot find it at home.*[31]

After a slow and difficult journey Lumumba finally took the train to Stanleyville. His arrival in the city marked a major transition in Lumumba's adult life. He became a civil servant and immersed himself in the social and cultural life of the city. Lumumba made Stanleyville his home and again became a public figure.

Stanleyville: Bright lights, big city

From Stanleyville the future looked bountiful. A rail link was opened connecting the copper-rich province of Katanga and South Africa. Diamond mining expanded and by 1930 the Congo was responsible for the production of at least half of the world's industrial diamonds. Cotton was promoted by the colonial state as a profitable export crop, production began in 1917 and within 16 years there were 700,000 planters across the country. By the mid 1940s the Congo produced 73 per cent of the world's cobalt and 15 per cent of the world's copper supply.[32]

By 1940 Congolese society had entered a period of 'modernisation'; it was a society that was thoroughly globalised. Its products, produced specifically for export, were bought all over the world. In the Congo there was the rudimentary development of an education system. For those employed in modern companies in the new cities of the Congo there was also a certain level of healthcare and access to housing. Although the roads and rail links were built for commercial reasons, to export crops and raw materials to ports and cities in the region, they made it possible to cross the Congo relatively easily. Perhaps we can detect a certain progress in the lives of some Congolese, certainly when compared to their miserable conditions at the turn of the century.

Some of this 'progress' can be charted in the access to schooling. In 1950, no African child could attend a European school. However later in the decade, pending the successful inspection of the child's family, a black child might be allowed to attend a European school. So by 1958 10 per cent of the children at European schools were Congolese.[33] Still, the old Congo remained and as late as 1955 men in rural areas were obliged to provide unpaid labour to the state.

Early struggles

Colonial rule in the Congo determined the nature of resistance. There was a specific violence unique to the Belgian Congo. Tony Busselen explains that 'the colonial system in the Congo was brutal and repressive not only physically but with psychological violence. So throughout the history of the Congo you have moments of popular explosion and then periods of extraordinary obedience and apparent calm.'[34] The most effective 'explosion' was the millenarian campaign of 1921 led by Simon Kimbangu, who became a prophet to those who followed him in the area around Nkamba. Kimbangu drew towards him those who were attracted to the idea of a native church. Though he did not raise the banner of 'independence', he acted as a conduit to a wider discontent, and urban workers and rural peasants flocked to his movement. Threatened by the possibility of a more widespread rebellion the Belgian colonial administration attempted to arrest Kimbangu, forcing him to go into hiding. After weeks on the run he conceded defeat and handed himself in. Deported to Katanga, he was sentenced to death. But fearing a backlash from his supporters, and mindful of earlier resistance, the administration commuted the sentence to life imprisonment.

Resistance was not limited to religious movements. The 'war effort' sped up processes that saw the formation of a Congolese working class, and the new industry gave rise to new forms of organised struggle. One dramatic example was in November 1941, when miners at Jadotville, Kipushi, Likasi, Luisha and foundrymen in Elisabethville (Lubumbashi) started to organise something like a general strike. In the evening of 3 December 1941, workers at the Shituru and Pandotville factories in Jadotville unanimously agreed to go out on strike. In an effort to agitate for a wider strike workers travelled to the surrounding areas of Likasi, Luishia and Kambove.

This was an impressive movement. Though frequently described as a miner's strike, it actually involved factory workers, railwaymen, watchmen and informal traders: a shifting constellation of skilled and unskilled workers together with informal traders. When the strike reached Elisabethville the government panicked; this was after all the major profit centre for the Congo. More soldiers were sent for. Workers were promised a 30 per cent increase. This offer did not break the strike so the authorities finally resorted to violence, some suggesting that as many as 100 demonstrators were killed.[35]

This strike was only one of several. Between 1941 and 1947, strikes in Katanga were common. Other action appears even more radical: between February and May 1944, soldiers attempted an insurrection in Katanga. The broad nature of the movement's demands gives a sense of its radicalisation: an end to starvation, the end to forced labour, the abolition of corporal punishment in the prisons and racial epithets in the army and at work. Again the movement was defeat by a wave of repression.

The 1939–45 war prompted calls for African liberation. Ostensibly the war was being fought against fascism, so how could the continuation of racial and colonial divisions be justified? Some 15,000 Congolese soldiers served during the war in Palestine and across Europe with their white counterparts. Once the war was over they returned to the Congo to be treated as colonial subjects. This created enormous frustration amongst them.

Stanleyville

In was in this context of expanding opportunities (and of resistance) that Lumumba arrived in Stanleyville, now aged about 20. He stayed with Paul Kimbulu. Kimbulu was not a member of his family but was know and respect by the Batetelas in the city. Lumumba introduced himself as someone from Onalua, and he was warmly welcomed into the family home.

Setting up in Stanleyville was complicated and demeaning for most Congolese. Strict racial segregation was practised. Workers were kept in compounds and denied access to white areas. When whites kept blacks as domestic servants they did not let them have a room in their house, but kept them in huts outside, and many were kept locked in them at night. Education was restricted. Social centres, including restaurants, theatres and the cinema, closed their doors to Africans, even those who could afford to pay.

Juliana Lumumba describes the segregation of the Belgian Congo: 'When you reached 18 years old you had to carry a permit, which would indicate what you did. If you were stopped, you had to justify why you were in town. If you were a domestic servant, then you would be allowed to continue on your way. Even today you will notice that people refer to the "*cité*", this is where black people lived, while the whites lived in town. There were also curfews, so after 6 o'clock if you were not working you did not have the right to move around. And if a black man looked at a white woman, he could find himself in prison.'[36]

A 'transfer permit' was demanded by the colonial authorities for those who wanted to move to urban centres. Lumumba had arrived without authorization from the region of Katako-Kombe. Admission was controlled by the *Centre Extra-Coutumier* (CEC) – literally, and somewhat obscurely, 'Extra-Traditional Centres' – who attempted to slow down the rural exodus.

The CEC made all the decisions in Stanleyville. For example from 1942 to 1943 the council admitted 110 candidates out of 275 requests. The black population of Stanleyville at the time was approximately 25,000.[37] Even with control of rural migration the colonial authorities were nervous. The Centre's main preoccupation was the control of 'desirables' and the ejection of 'undesirables'. To do this they divided the native population between 'professional unemployed', 'parasites', people living 'without funds', and 'boys deemed unsatisfactory' (domestic servants). But the Centre was riven with contradictions. Prostitutes were admitted without hesitation, because they paid their taxes and represented an important source of revenue for the Centre. For most of those admitted on temporary 'passports', a signed contract for work with a minimum duration of one year was required, or more frequently permits were issued where the holder had to find work within eight days.

Lumumba stayed with Paul Kimbulu for several years. Kimbulu had five children in the house at the time of Lumumba's arrival. Lumumba, he later said, became his sixth child. Lumumba quickly integrated himself into the household. Forever curious, he was always interested in whatever Kimbulu read, and occasionally they conversed in French, Lumumba pressing him to recount stories of what happened before he came to Stanleyville. 'I found him curious about everything, always respectful. He was also amusing, bringing together the children and our wives to organize family games. Lumumba played the tam-tam and sang.'[38] He would bring his friends to the house or on the weekends they would organise excursions out of the city on bicycles, often returning with fish they had caught. Kimbulu became a father figure, who unlike Lumumba's own father was not authoritarian.

The postman

Lumumba was a resident of Stanleyville until 1956. For most of this time he worked for the colonial postal service. By late November 1944 Lumumba started to work as a clerk with the post office. His office was close to both the School of the Marist Brothers (*Ecole des Freres Maristes*), where he would attend evening classes. When he was first employed he was single, and received a monthly salary of 150 Belgian francs, with an additional sum for housing. He also had the right to basic medical care. When

Lumumba married almost a year later, his salary increased by 15 francs. His first two years in the postal service seemed to have past without incident. He took his new position seriously and by mid-1947 he had obtained permission to pursue a course at the Post Office School of Léopoldville (*Ecole Postale de Léopoldville*).

From 1944 Lumumba intensified his efforts to improve his education. He had left Onalua with only rudimentary schooling, and still struggled to write and express himself in French. Stanleyville tantalised him with its possibilities; of work but also self-improvement. There was an array of courses taught in colleges and schools, as well as a library that gave him an opportunity that he had never before had to study and read. So began his lifelong obsession with reading. Whenever he could not be found it was fair to assume that he was buried in a book in the public library.

Lumumba had a keen sense of the struggle he faced to 'improve' himself. This effort at self-education was a defining one. In a letter to his friend Emile Luhahi in 1954 he reflected on his trajectory and the plans he still had to pursue further learning. *You asked me about my future and my projects … I have many projects which are centred on one ideal: to have a thorough education … because for me wealth has no value. I prefer to have a competent education than to be rich, ignorant. Whether I go to university or not, I have to divide myself into four parts to become a man relatively informed to better serve my homeland. At college they only give us instruments, it is my responsibility to use these instruments in a way that they can become precious tools. What are these instruments? It is a basic knowledge that we were taught on our school benches …*

I can affirm, dear Emile, that one can become a true college man, that is to say acquire a quasi-university training – if not at university – <u>even staying at home</u> … What is my educational experience? Certainly you know it … It is certainly thanks to my own effort, my perfectionism, my perseverance.

Today even Europeans characterise me as formidable. A European friend said to me one day: 'In European circles everyone says Lumumba wants to impose his intellectual superiority as much on the Congolese as the whites'. This idea comes from burning polemics that I have had with the Europeans, polemics for which I have come out victorious. Here in Stan, all the Congolese take me for a magician ...the Europeans take me for a man of superior education. Lots of Europeans, including my Head of Department, asserts that I am better educated than many Europeans.

As you know since last year it has been a question whether I pursue my education at university. I was admitted to the University of Kimuenza ... but ... there is not yet accommodation for married students – I will have to divorce so I can become single!!! ... Anyway I have not lost confidence. Either I will go to university, or I will enrol in courses by correspondence for the same kind of studies, this is what I have already started ... at the Centre of Higher Studies in Brussels (Centre d'Etudes Superieures de Bruxelles).[39]

Lumumba left Stanleyville in July 1947 for the capital. Created in 1946 the Post Office School sought to train Congolese postal workers in all postal functions. The school recruited roughly 40 students per year from the Congo's six provinces. Lumumba had just been awarded his primary school certificate in Stanleyville when he was accepted.

The course took nine months and included instruction on letters, parcels, cheques and the geography of the Congo and Belgium. Lumumba came third in a class of 34 in the final exam in March 1948. After completing his training in Léopoldville Lumumba was appointed a 3rd grade clerk, in the service of Post and Telecommunications. His salary increased to 1,500 francs, and he also acquired the use of a bicycle and a housing allowance.

Léopoldville was important to him for another reason. Across the river from the city was the French colonial city of Brazzaville. Lumumba visited the city and was struck immediately by how little it had of Léopoldville's harsh racism and segregation. He was impressed: *Africans under French administration move around without hindrance, hold important posts and send deputies to the National Assembly in Paris.*[40] The Belgian Congo was, in contrast, an empire of silence.

The obedient clerk of Stanleyville was becoming more forceful. His first open quarrel with the authorities came in December 1948. On the 8 December he wrote to the head of provincial finances, disputing the change in his salary after a temporary transfer. *I draw to your attention to the fact that my housing and bicycle allowances can be maintained as I am in the same conditions of service as Stanleyville …I am asking you to inform me on the subject of the reduction of my payments.*[41]

Léopoldville would not have disappointed Lumumba. It was an extremely modern city, with skyscrapers, air-conditioned restaurants, hotels and a modern transport system. The city had the largest stadium on the continent holding 75,000 people. There was even a whiff of the *avant garde* about the capital. In the 1950s the colonial administration experimented with the *gyrobus*, an electric bus more advanced than anything being used in Europe at the time.

Under other circumstances this polite query into a change of salary and allowances, would have been dealt with reasonably. The response of the deputy director of finances was vicious. He explained that the calculation of Lumumba's salary was not the result of an error and he repeated that the housing allowance and bicycle had been withdrawn. He then let out a nasty riposte: 'henceforth do not bother me with these absurd concerns, lacking of any interest.' Lumumba was not deterred. He replied at the end of December: *Seen as my bike is only used in the interests of work and that the distance between my lodgings and the office justifies it, I am appealing to you to revisit the question and that my allowances are maintained.*[42]

From now on Lumumba would not be intimidated by his white bosses, nor would he accept their edicts if he regarded them as unjust. These were not revolutionary demands but important challenges to his white employers. The following years were marked

An aerial view of a boulevard in central Léopoldville in 1959

by similar complaints, often disputes about irregularities in his salary, loans and allowances. Lumumba had a growing sense of unease at the racism inherent in colonialism.

On 5 February 1954 Lumumba was notified that he had been recorded in the 'Register of the civilised indigenous population'. To achieve the status of *registered* in the Belgian Congo, each aspiring *évolué* was obliged to jump through certain hoops. Juliana describes these trials: 'To be *évolué* in the 1950s you had to prove you were "evolved" – that you were suitably civilised. I once asked my parents what this meant. It was a deeply humiliating process. You would be given a test, someone would come to the house and see if you had an inside toilet, if your children wore pyjamas, if you ate with a knife and fork – only then would you be given the accreditation "*évolué*". You were then allowed to enter certain whites-only shops. .. which were normally barred for Africans. So the status "*évolués*" gave you certain advantages in relation to the rest of the population.'[43] Lumumba had become an important figure within the group of *évolués* in Stanleyville. In April 1956 the Governor General Léo Pétillon asked Lumumba to form part of a Congolese delegation to Belgium in April and May that year.

The terms *évolué* was used to designate an urbanised and educated layer of Africans, meaning literally 'evolved'. The *évolués* were identified by the white authorities as being 'more like us', and superior to the mass of colonised society. As junior civil servants the *évolués* helped to run the colonial state. One conduit towards joining this privileged elite was the school system: the more diplomas you acquired the more 'evolved' you became.

Wives, lovers and children

Lumumba was married traditionally to three women; these women were Henriette Maletaua, Hortense Sombosia and Pauline Opango. He also had two lovers, Pauline Kia and Alphonsine Masuba. The first marriage was to Henriette Maletaua about a year after he had arrived in Stanleyville. She stayed with Lumumba until 1947. They had no children. It was with his second partner, Hortense Sombosia, that he had a more durable and serious relationship. Married according to custom in June 1947 by February 1951 the couple were divorced, again having no children.

It was with Pauline Kia, who he never married, that he seems to have the most enduring relationship. She was a confident and precocious woman, who could stand up to her partner. Early in her life she had moved to Léopoldville with her father, who had worked for the Office of Congolese Transport (*Office des Transport Congolais*), where she was sent to school. The couple met for the first time in the capital in 1947 during Lumumba's stay in the city while he trained at the Post Office School. It was here that they become lovers. Pauline was an experienced woman, and already a mother of a small girl. Lumumba and Pauline were forced to separate when her parents left Léopoldville.

But in 1948 they met again in Stanleyville. Before long she managed to supplant both Lumumba's circles of friend and his legal wife, Hortense. She remembered years later that 1950 was the moment of their deepest love, their *bolingo makasi* ('strong love' in Lingala). On 20 September 1951 she gave birth to François, Lumumba's first child. They were in every practical sense husband and wife. Recalling her 'husband' years later she remembered that he 'drank lots of coffee in the morning, afternoon and evening, normally without sugar or milk, he carefully cleaned his clothes, went out little … because he was absorbed by his interminable reading and correspondence.' They might not have gone out much on the weekend but they entertained 'we had to prepare for our visitors… it was very tiring.'[44]

The relationship came to an end in 1951. The arrival of his new wife, in an arranged marriage from Wembo-Nyama in March 1951, reinforced the separation. Pauline Kia returned to Léopoldville with her son. But this was not the end of their relationship; on the contrary they kept in close contact and Lumumba was determined not to lose touch with his son. Pauline explained, 'Despite this separation I continued to receive money from Patrice to help with the child. Many of his friends came to see me, instructed by him to do so.'[45] In 1954 he wrote to his friend Emile Luhahi with instructions to find out about his son:

I am very pleased to learn of your departure for Léopoldville … If you can please visit my much loved son, François Hemery Flory, now three years, who is in Léopoldville with his mother Mme Pauline Nkiele… Find out what state you find the child and give me his news as soon as you can. If you can be photographed with him as a souvenir: two different photographs, one together and one with him alone. I will send you the money to buy the photographs. It is very important! Do not lose sight of this!!! I am impatiently waiting. He is my first child that I had with a woman of Léopoldville.[46]

But there was more to the continued contact than this. Lumumba remained deeply attached to his ex-lover. Pauline Kia kept in contact with him until the end. 'At the time of his arrest in 1960 I went to see him several times, first in the military camp of Binza and afterwards in Thysville where he would be transferred. With the complicity of certain soldiers … I disguised myself in military clothes … I still love my husband.'[47]

Pauline Opango was Lumumba's most significant relationship, even if it was not always an easy or happy one. Married in 1951 she would stay with Lumumba until his death and have four children with him: Patrice who was born on 18 September 1952, Juliana born on 23 August 1955 and Roland-Gilbert born in 1958 and a girl, Marie-Christine, who died several months after her birth in 1960. Although dates are not precise Pauline Opango Onosamba was born in approximately 1937, in Wembo-Nyama. She was little more than a child bride. When they married they had not previously met. Lumumba's younger brother Emile presented the Opango family with the dowry: a goat, cloth and a little money.

Pauline and Patrice Lumumba photographed with their children Patrice and Juliana during their few months residence in the Prime Minister's villa in Léopoldville. 1 August 1960

Opango recalled the day of her marriage more than 40 years later, 'I was wearing an elegant dress, European style. Before Patrice's family came to see us, my mother told me that I was going to marry a man in Stanleyville … She told me that the man was handsome and good. I was happy, but truth be told, I was too young to understand.' Soon after the wedding she joined Lumumba in Stanleyville. Still a child, she had to learn how to clean the house, take care of herself and dress correctly. 'My husband and my sister [who already lived in Stanleyville] had to teach me everything.' Lumumba was often out, and returned late. When he was at home he spent most of his time consumed by his books. For the young Pauline, used to the familiarity of her village, this would have been a strange new life indeed. Unlike Kia they did not argue in public, but the relationship was hard for both of them. Writing to Emile in 1954 he expressed his doubts. *Turning to my wife. She admitted that she had aborted by categorically refusing to look after herself. She repeats often that she does not want any more children.*[48]

She arrived in Lumumba's household a child, and began to see the marriage as a burden. But each time she resolved to leave, her elder sister, who lived in the city, would convince her to stay. Finally Pauline left Stanleyville in April 1952 after a domestic quarrel. She returned to her parents in Wembo-Nyama, where she gave birth to Patrice. Lumumba was accompanying a study group to the region, his first trip home since he had left in 1943, and visited his new-born son. Initially Lumumba thought he would return alone to Stanleyville, confirming the separation. But after long negotiations they returned together in January 1953. In 1955 they had their second child, Juliana.

Alphonsine Masuba was Lumumba's last lover. They met for the first time in 1960. She worked as his secretary. Of all his partners Alphonsine was perhaps the closest to Lumumba intellectually. She understood his work, could arrange his library and knew the reasons for long absences. She had a child by Lumumba, a son Guy, who was born after his father's murder.

But without doubt Pauline Opango was the central female figure in his life, with her he had most of his children and spent many years. Pauline was a determined partner, even if she did not understand her husband's political convictions. Their daughter Juliana Lumumba explains that it was inevitable that there were certain problems in her parents' relationship, most of which she attributes to her mother's youth. 'My parents were very young; when my father died he was 36 years old. My mother was a widow at 28. It was a partnership that had all the problems of marrying at such a young age, and with a couple who often didn't see much of each other. She knew that he was totally preoccupied by politics and that our house was open to everyone. I don't think that they had any more problems than this … my mother has never remarried, she never wanted to. She had an enormous amount of love for her husband.'[49]

What sort of man does this make Lumumba? He had three wives, one a child-bride who he could not understand, all within a six-year period from 1945. The marriages were often an attempt to find an acceptable way of living with a partner in the tightly controlled community of Stanleyville. But Lumumba also had to straddle two worlds, and sought acceptance in both. There was the rural one of his family in Onalua, who found him a bride, and insisted repeatedly that he stay with her. In addition there was the urban one, of the *évolués* and the prospect of social advance. Lumumba sought to negotiate both. He was also becoming a public figure, who participated in political and cultural discussions in the city. In managing these two, distinct universes, there were contradictions in his behaviour. In the perfect and educated Congo that he envisaged in the 1950s he was the enlightened liberal, seeing women in a much more prominent position, even if they did not always play this role in his household.

Early on he championed the rights of Congolese women: *Responsibility for the backwardness of women falls on the husbands ... A large number of Congolese husbands care little for the education of their wives, whom they regard – and this symbolises the ancestral ideas which are still strongly held by many Africans – not as their companions and their closest friends, but as servants whose function in the home is only to bear children, to enrich the clan, to prepare meals for the army of lazy parasites who are continually sponging on the household ... Can we honestly claim to be évolué when we leave our wives and children to eat on the ground like savages whilst we ourselves eat at tables?*[50]

Lumumba was anxious to make his household, despite the evident difficulties, a model for the community in which he was a rising star. In 1955 for example at an event organized by the governor of the *Province Orientale* in honor of the Belgium monarch King Baudouin's official visit to the Congo, Lumumba brought his pregnant wife. Most *évolués* came alone.

There seems no doubt that Lumumba loved all of his children. Initially he only wanted a couple, so he could educate them thoroughly. But when children came he accepted all of them, and according to some accounts he regretted not having had the chance for more. He was heavily involved in his children's education; Juliana remembers that he refused any magical charms to protect his children. He did not allow Pauline to use them, and was furious when she bought them into the house. Lumumba wrote from personal experience about this: *In the teeth of the opposition of their évolué husbands, some wives will insist on their children wearing these good-luck charms which preserve babies against evil.*[51]

Juliana has vivid memories of her father: 'When I was small I was very close to him... I was often in his office. He worked enormously hard, and I would watch him work, rewriting or practising a speech. My father was a very affectionate person, when he was with us he always chatted and played. Of course he was busy and he was often absent, but when he was there, he was *really* there. I remember that when he came back late, he would always come and see me. He was available to us, present. He bought up his children. My mother didn't want us to call him "Patrice", so he was always "papa".'[51] His eldest son François explains that although he did not have much time to spend with his family, 'the little time that he had he tried to make us understand why he was often absent'.[52] Education for his children was vital for Lumumba: *Children are not like mushrooms which grow at random. Education in the home is the most valuable and lasting form of education which any man can have. The school can do no more than supplement and improve it.*[54] He also insisted that his children attend the Royal Athenaeums, which were European schools that had recently been established in the Congo.

According to Batetela custom, each child at birth should take the name of a relative or a friend. Patrice, breaking with tradition, named them all simply 'Lumumba'. He was the exemplary modern man, pulling disparate pieces of a new and old world together to make a fresh identity. His children would be drawn into his cosmopolitan world.

Congolese intelligentsia

Those who rose to positions of importance were a new group of Congolese men, who had been trained by the Belgians to work at junior levels of the colonial apparatus. These sub-contractors for the colonial state were clerks, low-level civil servants and even certain soldiers. Though the colonial state systematically discriminated against the Congolese, the growth of the economy created a certain space through which some Congolese could emerge. So in 1953, for example, there were 463 Africans from this new category in Léopoldville, who could afford their own car. One writer described a 'new class', seeing this group of Congolese men campaigning for national liberation.[55]

George Nzongola-Ntalaja details the involvement of *évolués* in the struggle for independence. He argues that it 'was basically a continuation of their fight for equality of opportunity in the colonial political economy', he writes, 'where they experienced discrimination with respect to career and other economic opportunities, in addition to the daily humiliations of colonial racism.' Between 1958 and 1960 the collective experience of discrimination drew this group closer to the urban and rural poor. The growth of this class can be seen in the number of friendly associations, clubs and societies that were set up. By 1956 there were 313 such clubs in the Congo, with a membership of 15,000. Still the process was extremely uneven, so as late as 1960, there was only one Congolese citizen with a law degree.[56] Little space was ever permitted by the Belgian state for the formation of a separate class of intellectuals.

Busselen describes the reality of life for Congolese *évolué*: 'You would not find a single book on Marxism in 1958 in the whole of the country. You could go to a seminary to become a priest but otherwise there was nothing else. The training for the *évolué* involved finding a white family who would tutor you on how to eat and dress. This was the environment.'[57] If the limited progress that had been made in the previous 20 years had been accompanied with the removal of racial barriers, there might have been larger numbers arguing for a continuation of Belgian rule in another form. But the experience of repeated racial humiliation drove Belgium's natural allies to take more radical positions.

The role of this class was certainly not unique to the Congo. Tony Cliff writing in 1963 offers perhaps the clearest analysis of the role of the 'intelligentsia' in the movements for independence. He maintained that the failure of the working class to lead the movements for national independence and democracy in the Third World was due to the relative inexperience of this class. The leadership of nationalist struggles was taken up by a '*petit bourgeois*' student-intelligentsia. The lack of organisation among the working class was in contrast to the high level of political and organisational coherence among a specialised group of intellectuals. In the Congo this was the *évolué*.[58] In a biography of Lumumba Cliff's model serves as a powerful description of how change actually occurred in the Congo.

The Congolese elite possessed no capital of their own, major mining companies and businesses were owned by foreign companies. Only in the 1950s had the *évolués* even been granted the right to own their own houses. Most were employees themselves, as clerks and administrators in the colonial state. While the Congolese elite had a thirst for wealth, they were not involved in the ownership and production of it. One study of the Congo described the situation for the black elite at independence: 'the profitable sectors of the economy were already cornered by foreign … corporations. Therefore all that they could sell was their political power and influence in the state machinery.'[59] Though the *évolué* may have helped to lead the struggle for independence most members of this class were happy to accept their subordinate role as recipients of foreign capital. Lumumba's early writing expressed the aspirations of this class.

The first generation of post-independent leaders were often serious scholars. A 'presidential-intelligentsia' ran many parts of the continent. Kenya's first head of state, Jomo Kenyatta, was the country's first black 'anthropologist'. Uganda's Milton Obote changed his name to honour John Milton the author of the epic English poem *Paradise Lost*. While Julius Nyerere in Tanzania is famous for his writings on 'African socialism', he is less well known for his Kiswahili translations of *Julius Caesar* and *The Merchant of Venice* for Oxford University Press.

Columnist and student

Lumumba's transformation from a barely literate new resident of Stanleyville to established writer was phenomenal. Lumumba's spoken French at the dawn of his urban life was basic, his written

French even more rudimentary. He undertook a regime of intensive self-education, following French courses in the evening at the School of the Marist Brothers and in 1948, when he had already mastered much of the language, he enrolled in a correspondence course. On top of this he plunged himself into a programme of extensive reading at a library where he worked as a volunteer. By mid-1948 he was a graduate of the Post Office School, and was now among the most educated Congolese of the period, with a level of French that exceeded many Europeans in the colony. All this he achieved in less than four years.

It was not until 1950, when Lumumba was 25 years old, that he began to write regularly in Congolese newspapers, reviews and later Belgian publications. *The Cross of the Congo* (*La Croix du Congo*) was a Catholic paper published in Léopoldville, *Africa and the World* (*L'Afrique et le Monde*) was a monthly review published in Brussels and *The Voice of the Congolese* (*La Voix du Congolais*) was a monthly paper that was published especially for the *évolués* and produced by the Information Service for the colony. He was also editor-in-chief of the *Echo Postal*, a publication set up specifically for African postal workers in the province.

What did Lumumba write about? His chief concerns seem to have been the lives of the *évolués*, minor colonial officials like himself. Throughout this period Lumumba wrote repeatedly about the importance of improving the lives of the *évolués*, to bring them closer to the cultural values and behaviour of Europeans. During this period Lumumba was not overly concerned with the miserable lot of the mass of Congolese.

There was also a certain missionary zeal in much of his writing in this period, constantly correcting the behaviour of members of his circle. Lumumba's writing was heavily instructive, and his model was the superior civilisation that had colonised the Congo. The words that came up again and again in his work reflected this penchant: perseverance, ideals, progress.

Lumumba was the educator *par excellence*, not only for his community, but for the restricted membership of the *évolués*. So at the age of 31 he encouraged his fellow educated Congolese to join him in the library; *I am, myself, the librarian of a large library which has been opened in the centre of a large province, but you will be amazed to learn that there are not more than ten regular readers, and that often several weeks go by without a single reader. The books, supplied regularly by the Government, are mouldering.*[60] Lumumba became one of the principle defenders of schooling in Stanleyville. He dreamt of going to university in Lovanium, near the capital Léopoldville and then to the Free University of Brussels, but he knew he could not fulfil the conditions. Still he was jubilant on the behalf of the Congolese community in Stanleyville, when an admissions board was established in the city in 1953.

Lumumba was far from a radical voice in town. In July 1952 he assisted his friend Paul Fabo on a conference debating the 'collaboration between whites and blacks'. Lumumba wrote a report on the conference, and used the opportunity to advise the *évolués* to learn and work, not to depend on whites, but to collaborate with them and to understand that their role was to act as intermediaries between the masses and the European civilising mission. But the conference was also the opportunity for more radical dissension from the colonial project. While the speakers were extolling the virtues of the coloniser, dissent could be heard from the floor. One participant criticised a speaker, exclaiming 'the overwhelming majority of Europeans seem to have come here not to civilise us but to enrich themselves.' Fabo was forced to admit that there were cases like this but these 'were rare'.[61] Lumumba did not stray from Fabo's snub of the participant.

Lumumba campaigned against the apartheid-like segregation between Europeans and the Congolese. But these 'campaigns' were limited to those he regarded as civilised; the Congolese who had achieved a suitable degree of education and cultivation. His was not a project of universal equality, but a *Belgian-Congolese Union where whites and blacks will discuss without clashing the problems of today*.[61] He pestered the government in his columns and articles to allow the Congolese free access to public places that were reserved for Europeans.

Lumumba defended the colonial mission started by Stanley on the 50th anniversary of his death. The article – though it was more of a study, covering seven pages – appeared in *The Voice of the Congo* in May 1954. The piece did not limit itself to the events of Stanley's life, but the entire project of European colonialism in the Congo. In contrast to the great sacrifices and civilisation of the Europeans, who first penetrated the region, pre-colonial Congo was a savage and dangerous place. After describing the brutality of Africa, Lumumba went on to eulogise the humanitarian work of Stanley and King Léopold II.

The deliverance from fear ... this freedom of life, this sense of human dignity: is it not to Stanley and Léopold II that we owe it? Who delivered us from famines, devastating epidemics? Was it not Stanley and Léopold?... Stanley gave us peace, rendered us our human dignity, improved our physical existence, instructed our intelligence, developed our souls.

Their sacrifice has not been wasted and...has ...placed Belgium among the great colonial powers, and us, the natives, among the underdeveloped populations the better colonised.[63]

But it would be wrong to see his writings as simply one-dimensional, always praising colonialism, always sycophantic to the authorities. His persisted in arguing that while the colonisers had come to civilise the Congo, both Europeans and the Congolese were equal. *Whether you are registered or not, black or white, yellow or red, we all have the same value and the same human dignity ... we are all descendants from a common ancestor*.[64] Still it is hard to escape the sense that Lumumba was responding to the exclusion of the small and privileged group of Congolese *évolués*, who were simultaneously promoted and excluded by the colonial administration.

Lumumba suffered personally from the discrimination of the colonial state that he championed in his writings. One incident took place with his close friend, Pierre Clément. Clément was a French anthropologist working in the Congo. He collaborated extensively with Lumumba in this period and they became close friends. Later he wrote about Lumumba's personality which 'harmoniously integrated intelligence, will, courage, spirit of enterprise, tenacity, curiosity … he has a power to work, vitality and … he is apparently tireless.'[65] In 1952 Lumumba joined Clément on a research trip to his home region. Lumumba was humiliated when they boarded a boat together and were then forced to separate into racially demarcated seating. On another occasion in Leopoldville Lumumba collided with a white woman, who screamed at him: 'Dirty monkey! Can you not see where you are going?'[66] He began to argue that this type of discrimination and racism must end.

For such a capacious reader it is perhaps surprising that Lumumba was ignorant of Marxism and socialism but these gaps in his knowledge are in large part descriptive of Congolese society. Strict censorship limited the choice of books at Lumumba's disposal, though at the time he was a stern moralist and model for members of his community.

After independence Lumumba was condemned for being a communist sympathiser, despite the fact that he had little knowledge of what communism really meant. His friend and collaborator Jean Van Lierde explained that Lumumba 'had not read ten lines of Marx, Engels or Lenin, he preferred Martin Luther King, Ghandhi … he did not have any communist training.' For Lumumba the notion of class struggle was a dangerous idea imported from the north that could only serve to divide a fragile national unity. Why add this divisive concept, he asked, when there was already the potential of ethnic division in the Congo?

Lumumba's writing, though often sycophantic to colonialism, was marked by persistent requests for the improvements in the lives of the *évolués*. Eventually he would lose his admiration for Belgian colonialism but not his restless insistence for justice. From 1958 the equality he sought was no longer limited to a privileged group. The training that he had received in Stanleyville, as a writer, postman and public figure, was vital to his future trajectory. This was particularly true of his involvement in the associations and clubs in Stanleyville.

Association des Évolués de Stanleyville

Stanleyville was a hive of clubs, associations and community groups long before Lumumba arrived in the city. But the officially sanctioned associations had a particular history of their own. The state sought to record and legislate for every aspect of life in the colony, so when associations began to be formed so did the laws to go with them. A stream of ordinances gave powers to the authorities to control and organise associations.

The most important of these associations was the Association of *Évolués* of Stanleyville (AES). The colonial state was quick to see the importance of promoting the *évolué*. In 1948 the 'civic merit card' was introduced, and then in 1952 another decree bought into existence formal registration (*immatriculation*), which was the recognition of eminent Congolese citizens. Lumumba described how registration *is an instrument by which certain Congolese are assimilated with non-natives in regard to their civil status by being made subject to civil laws of the European pattern ... the immediate aim ... is to grant the benefits of immatriculation only to those of the native elite who have genuinely adopted the Western form of civilisation.*[67] Lumumba's 'registration' in 1954 was celebrated in the Congolese press. The number of Congolese who were actually of registered status remained incredibly low: in the first three years of the decree only 116 Congolese had been admitted.

The AES was authorised on 28 October 1944 by the head of the district, who had long wanted to create an association of clerks. There was also a military reason. That year marked the end of the intense phase in the war which had seen an important expansion in the responsibilities of colonial clerks and junior members of the regional and national state. The state's decision to establish formal organisations for a specific category of *évolués* was in part an attempt to meet the aspirations of a class of colonial workers who had seen their workload and responsibilities increase. It was also a conscious attempt to separate this group from the Congolese masses. The first president of the AES made the objectives of the association clear: 'Our association is not created with the aim of forming a group of revolutionaries nor of recalcitrants, on the contrary its principle aim is to contribute to the general interests of the country.'[68]

The activities of the AES remained more or less unchanged over the next few years. Typical was a conference on the life of Stanley for the anniversary of his death and parties organised for the provincial governor, along with a test flight aboard the new DC3 of the Belgian airline Sabena. On 5 March 1954 Lumumba was elected president of the association, following public criticisms he made against the sitting president. But he did not limit himself to the AES. From 1953 Lumumba was the president or secretary of seven organisations in the city. By all accounts the election to the AES was an impressive operation that involved unseating the existing president while marginalising other candidates. This was Lumumba's first electoral triumph; just ten years after he had arrived in the city he led the most important association. In the absence of a real political life in the city Lumumba used his leadership in the associations to learn the mechanisms of political organisation. His first address as president of the AES gave no hint of a political project but it did argue for a widening out of the associations' activities, and emphasised the importance of cultural activities.

Within days of his election he was received by the governor of the province André Schöller. Lumumba raised five points, four of

King Baudouin and his Lord Chamberlain Count Gobert d'Aspremont Lynden leave the church of St Mary in Léopoldville after attending mass

these to do with housing. This was no accident. A house was the key to social standing, and the platform from which a member of the AES could present himself as respected and civilised. It was the crucial badge of civilisation. By the end of May Governor Schöller responded positively to all of Lumumba's requests. Lumumba scored his first triumph as president.

In June 1955 King Baudouin visited Stanleyville. By now Lumumba was a highly respected member of society. He was trusted enough to be introduced to the King on his visit to the city. At the reception held by the governor Lumumba managed to grab the King's attention and characteristically used the brief encounter to detail some of the complaints of the *évolués*. One of Lumumba's first biographers, Pierre de Vos, wrote a few years after the event that 'Baudouin seemed seduced by Lumumba who ... spoke with absolute frankness about the problems that confronted the *évolués*. .. The Post Office clerk, was also, seduced by his interlocutor who was the same age and, like him, was full of enthusiasm.'[69]

Lumumba was an impressive politician, maintaining links with important figures in the colonial authorities in the Congo and political figures he met from Belgium. In 1954 he met the new Minister of the Colonies Auguste Buisseret, a prominent member of the Liberal Party in Belgium and widely regarded as a reformer. He also became a member of the Liberal Study Circle (*Cercle libéral d'études*) which was affiliated to the Liberal Party. Buisseret eventually invited Lumumba to come to Belgium in 1956.

But Lumumba refused to do everyone's bidding. From 1954 he was repeatedly solicited by the members of the Catholic Church in Stanleyville to add the authority of the AES to complaints about the establishment of secular schools in the city. He refused. But it meant that Lumumba was forced to confront one of the central pillars of the colonial system: the Catholic Church. He commented two years later: *I personally have made myself unpopular by refusing to take part in these petty intrigues which I was asked to take part in and to lead.*[70]

Lumumba's position was suddenly challenged. Committee members attacked him for acting on behalf of the AES with no clear mandate. Lumumba was accused of using his authority as the leader of the AES to support secular education. By the beginning of 1956 accusations came quickly: he was accused of the 'abuse of power' and condemned for his 'dictatorial style', and two prominent members of the AES asked him to resign. The meeting with the King in June 1955 and the reception for Auguste Buisseret hosted by Lumumba in his home aroused further criticism. He was now condemned for his familiarity with the minister and inappropriate 'hand gestures' that accompanied a 'flood of words' when he had spoken with the King.

On 17 February 1956 Lumumba faced an unstoppable wave of opposition. He lost the election for president, winning only 16 votes. But this vote did not mark Lumumba's fall. In June 1956 Lumumba was lauded by the press for his public lectures on his visit to Belgium. However, his greatest challenge was to come and on 6 July he was arrested for embezzlement and imprisoned.

Embezzlement and prison

During Lumumba's study tour in Belgium an enquiry into his activities at the post office in Stanleyville was undertaken. Lumumba had been informed that such an enquiry might take place at the beginning of the year. The embezzlement amounted to withdrawing money from one account – a large shop, pharmacies or local businesses with accounts at the Post Office – and then repaying them through using money withdrawn from another account when they demanded payment. During interrogation in July 1956 Lumumba made it clear that he had always intended to repay the outstanding amounts. However, gradually they became too great, and his expenditure outpaced his ability to shift funds between accounts. From 1951 to 1954 the system of 'temporary withdrawals' had worked without being uncovered. But from 1954, along with Lumumba's changing status, his financial needs grew, leaving a regular deficit in the post office.

This last point is crucial. Promoted by the colonial state and expected to assume the responsibilities of a 'white' bureaucrat Lumumba still only received the miserly salary of a post office clerk. How could he be expected to entertain his white friends, receive visits from ministers and organise social activities on behalf of the AES if he was not adequately recompensed? The answer is that he could not. 'Creative accounting' was the only way Lumumba could maintain his status as a model member of the *évolués* in Stanleyville. As he wrote from prison: *How can a man improve his standard of living, secure decent conditions for his family, pay for his children's education and, in general, enter the ranks of the civilised, with such an inadequate income?*[71]

As soon as Lumumba realised that there was the possibility of an enquiry he stopped the withdrawals and started to reimburse the outstanding money. He decided to sell his house to ensure that he could pay back his debts. By June Lumumba had sold his house and was in the process of transferring money to the companies that were in deficit because of his withdrawals. At the time of his arrest Lumumba immediately confessed, admitted the 'irregularities' and expressed regret. *I want to be sincere. As I have said to my bosses, I committed some irregularities and I regret them.* When asked why he did this he made his motives clear. *Because I had financial difficulties. What I received in salary did not permit me to raise my three children, two of which go to the European school.*[72]

The reaction to his arrest in Stanleyville expressed many of the jealousies and suspicions that he had aroused. *Le Stanleyvillois* was the most naked in its condemnation of Lumumba. He was branded as a proud upstart who had committed grave errors. In the capital the daily newspaper *The Future* (*L'Avenir*) printed an article under the title 'Sad Incident' which expressed fury that a model of the community should have acted in such a despicable way.

Only Paul Fabo in *Africa and the World* defended Lumumba. He wrote at the end of July an article that exposed some of the real reasons why Lumumba had been treated so harshly. Fabo cited Lumumba's refusal to sign a petition opposing secular education in the Congo; 'having been received by the King and Minister of the colonies … the young and dynamic Patrice Lumumba, hope of young Congolese *évolués* … has been arrested and brutally thrown into prison …. We are well placed to say that Lumumba has been the victim of jealousy.'[73]

In prison Lumumba wasted no time. He pleaded to the authorities, wrote letters to Minister of the Colonies, to judges in Stanleyville and even to *his majesty Baudouin, King of the Belgians and the Congolese.* Many of the letters Lumumba sent in his first months in prison were concerned with his children and their future. Now that he was not working how could he possibility guarantee their schooling and well-being? Writing in August to the governor of the province André Schöller he expressed his worries: *My children are for the moment under the care of my brother who has two children of his own. Being momentarily unable to pay for their fees I would ask you if it would be possible to award them a study scholarship.*[73] In response to his insistence the authorities told him to send the children to his village of origin. Lumumba refused. He was determined that they could continue their education in a European school, where they could learn French and Western culture. *In the village their uncles and aunts would inculcate them with traditional customs contrary to the principles of European civilization in which I want to raise them ... if destiny has sadly separated me from my children just when their age demands serious care and attention to their moral education ... I ask the government of my country if it can ... look after the future of these registered children.*[75] As a result of Lumumba's persistence his children eventually received a grant and were able to continue their education in Stanleyville.

The apartheid divisions of the Belgian Congo continued in prison. As a registered *évolué* Lumumba received European privileges. The prison exemplified the idiocy of Belgian racial rule. There were distinct privileges for those Congolese who had passed the tests. Imprisoned Congolese who had been officially 'registered' were given 'toast, jam and butter' for breakfast and European meals for lunch and dinner. They could receive visitors, post and books and were given clean rooms.

It was in prison that Lumumba started to develop a critique of Belgian colonial rule: *Before the arrival of the European, no one had ever been detained in prison for a period of years or for the whole of his life. Offenders were punished expeditiously, and these old methods had a greater effect than the European methods. Our people have never known the outbreaks of offences which are prevalent in the Congo today, and this trend is continually increasing. Can it be that colonisation has led to a loosening of standards?*[76]

Lumumba could do the two things in prison that he was passionate about: read and write. The letters that he wrote concerning his case showed how he had mastered legal terms and the intricacies of colonial law. Although he was forbidden from publishing articles while in prison he managed to publish under the pen-name Boniface Lupaka. But Lumumba's main activity for the first five months was writing his only book, *The Congo land of the future is it threatened?* (*Le Congo terre d'avenir est-il menace?*). By December 1956 he had almost finished the book and wrote to the official Publicity Office (*Office de Publicité*) in Brussels asking if they would be interested in publishing it. In a letter to the official state publisher he explained the aims of the work: *to convey the ideas and aspirations of the Congolese people on various economic, social and political problems which are of particular concern to them … and on the solution of which – a happy solution, I hope – depend the future of the Congo and the success of Belgium's colonial mission … for the Belgian colonial mission has become the joint mission of Belgians and Congolese.*[77]

Several weeks later he received a request from the publisher to tell them something about himself. He wrote one of the few autobiographical notes known: *For more than six years I have been publishing articles dealing with the various social strata of the native population … Self-taught I have never stopped learning. At present I am studying law, philosophy, economics, social science, and administration … With regard to my family, I now have three children, of whom the two older attend school along with European children at the Stanleyville Royal Athenaeum.*[78]

The Publicity Office sent the manuscript for review. The reaction of one reviewer was vicious. The reviewer found the work to be a 'mix of cunning and naivety, of verbiage … and mad demands.' Strangely for a book that is noted for its moderation the reviewer criticised its radicalism 'the author wishes for nothing less that the equality of whites and blacks in every respect … As for the style, it will have to be seriously corrected. It is often in the style of the little negro'.[79] Finally Lumumba abandoned plans to get the book published.

Lumumba's 1956 book is a curious study. At the time it was condemned by supporters of Belgian colonialism as an audacious attack on the structures of the colonial state, but later it was also dismissed by many of Lumumba's supporters as hopelessly sycophantic towards the civilising mission of the Belgians. The book was initially rejected for publication but it was eventually printed in 1961 after his murder. The following year it was published in English under the title *Congo, my country*. Lumumba's comrades condemned its publication, believing that it gave an inaccurate picture of Lumumba's political ideas. In the same way Belgium hoped that its publication would tarnish Lumumba's martyrdom.

While Lumumba praises colonialism in the book – *It is thanks to Belgium that we are what we are: it is thanks to her that our country, risen from nothing only yesterday, is destined to rise in a few decades to the ranks of the civilised nations*[80] – these praises conceal a thorough critique. The book proposes systematic reforms of the Belgian Congo. Early in the book he insist on an end to flogging. Talking directly to the colonialist he explains *You do not win the confidence, respect or obedience of a subject people by wickedness, cruelty or harshness, but by good administration, respect for the rights of citizens and just and humane treatment.*[81] Nor is the book simply an appeal for the *évolués* Lumumba now saw himself as an advocate for the Congolese as a whole. On industrialisation and the division of wealth he is explicit: *The Congo is no longer a conquered colony to be exploited, where people come with the sole intention of filling their own pockets … what is the use of industrialising the Congo if it is to be mainly for the benefit of Europeans, whilst the labouring classes stagnate in relative poverty?*[81]

Belgian civilisation must not involve the denigration of African culture: *Do not destroy the African's soul by attempting to make the African a superficial caricature of a … black-skinned westerner.*[83]

Lumumba seems to have written the book in a frenzied rush, completing it in less than five months. His voice is raised repeatedly to condemn the exclusion of the *évolué* by colonialism racism, a humiliation that he must have felt personally, when a white *official speaks to us contemptuously in the second person singular … refuses to shake hands with us, receives us coldly in his office, or will not offer us a chair, as he would do to any European coming into a private or public office*. Lumumba was determined to warn the colonial state of the dangers that threatened the Congo unless there were urgent reforms. Lumumba was offering the Belgian Congo a last chance and in this sense the book was prophetic: *The more the natives are given the impression that their wishes are frustrated … the stronger will be their conviction that there is a desire to restrict their development. This will only rouse them and cause an increasing loss of confidence.*[84] Though Lumumba soon dropped the tone of gratitude in his writings and speeches, his political ideas can be traced clearly in the book.

Initially Lumumba was held under 'preventative detention', without being brought to court. By January 1957 he was still in prison waiting a trial. It was not until 25 February that he finally appeared in court. Lumumba was sentenced on 4 March 1957 but still his principal thoughts were with his children. He wrote on the same day a letter to the public prosecutor asking for an assurance that his children were fed and clothed correctly.

Sometimes the letters Lumumba wrote caused fury and indignation among colonial bureaucrats irritated no doubt by Lumumba's eloquence and confidence. One example was a detailed document written by Leon de Waersegger, Léopoldville's Chief Prosecutor, who was charged with handling Lumumba's case (and queries). His tone was vituperative. 'Lumumba is a Batetela from the region of Katako-Kombe … which was the theatre of Arab slave expeditions. It is in this region of the Congo that Belgium endured the hardest battles in the anti-slavery campaign where a large number of our countrymen paid with their blood for the liberation of the natives. Without our presence in the Congo what would Lumumba be? But if he owes the state for not being a slave, he also owes it for ... this education, this training which he boasts and that has been lavished on him completely free.'[85]

This is revealing. For the naked anger that it displays at the insolence of a 'liberated native' and as an example of the racism that existed in the Belgian Congo. Lumumba was, according to Waersegger, simply a Batetela native. White officials were convinced that the colonial mission had delivered Africans from slavery and barbarism, at the expense of white lives. If all of this was true how could the colonial state accept such unapologetic insistence from one of these freed slaves? Lumumba's crime was his audacity to even write to the colonial administration, let alone to question his detention.

Lumumba requested a move to Léopoldville, to be closer to the lawyer that he had engaged. He wanted to assist in the legal wrangling of his case. Lumumba was finally released on 7 September 1957, on condition that he found work immediately. The next day Lumumba was employed in the accounts department of a major brewery of the region. His salary, generous by Stanleyville standards, meant he would not need to juggle the books.

How can we understand Lumumba's development? His life already contained many of the contradictions of Belgian colonialism. His poor and rural childhood, where he acquired a rudimentary education in mission schools, was broken by an abrupt decision in the early 1940s to make his way to Stanleyville. By 1950 he had already become one of the leading figures in a group of educated Congolese in the city: a prolific writer, cultural organiser and moralist. Suddenly Lumumba was the quintessential urbanite, eloquent, charming and a model of everything that could be achieved in colonial Congo. But this moderate cheerleader for colonialism was to surprise everyone again. From 1957, after his spell in prison, Lumumba began to break with his old conciliatory self and emerge as a radical spokesperson for the independence of the Congo. With every new statement Lumumba made, each more adamant than the last, he was consciously distancing himself from his quiescent youth. His short life was the reversal of the adage that we become more moderate as we grow older. Experience would teach Lumumba a new radicalism and he would become the unswerving nationalist that he had always shunned. The contradictions in colonial life for the *évolués* could no longer hold. Lumumba's eldest son François explains that his father eventually 'revolted against the Europeans because he saw the contradictions between the ideas of a Belgium-Congo community and the reality of racism in the Congo.'[86]

Léopoldville: City of hope

While Lumumba had been in jail important changes were taking place in the Congo. Seemingly invulnerable to resistance, the whole structure of the colony caved in with remarkable speed. In 1955 Antoine van Bilsen, a Belgian professor, had seen independence in the distant future; his plan envisaged a 30-year transition to full independence for the Congo. Congolese and Belgian officials were told to look on the colony as a community linking two people, working together for the civilisation of Africa. Events in Léopoldville, Lumumba's new home, would crush these hopes.

The mood changed with astonishing speed in the Congo. But this change was external. In 1956 the British suffered a humiliating set-back in Egypt after their failure to recapture the Suez Canal. This triggered their rapid withdrawal from their African colonial empire. Colonel Nasser became a hero of the nationalist movement across the world, for his courage in standing up to British. Commenting on the threat of a British invasion Nasser said: 'I am not scared of these perfumed little soldiers from the British empire.' Though the French were more reluctant to follow, they were also forced to relinquish most of their African territories by 1960.

The Congo was a boom economy. Copper prices rose by 26 per cent between 1950–3. *Forbes* magazine in 1952 praised the Congo commenting that it was an investors' paradise. A survey of dozens of Belgian companies operating in the Congo revealed massive profit rates between 15 per cent and an extraordinary 21 per cent.[87] As we have seen this expansion saw the contradictory growth of a new class of educated Congolese, who increasingly made demands on the state, but it also led to the determination by Belgium to hold on to the Congo at all costs.

Beer and politics in Léopoldville

Life in Stanleyville was over for Lumumba. It was the site of his extraordinary rise to prominence, but also of his falling prey to petty jealousies and intrigue. He saw his life and the possibility of resuscitating his future in the capital. Politically Léopoldville had been transformed by the *'plan de 30 ans'* (30-year plan), which envisaged independence after a long period of education and training for the Congolese. One political organization, the *Alliance des Bakongo* (ABAKO), was now leading a political struggle in the open. Léopoldville, after the claustrophobic restrictions of Stanleyville, must have been a revelation. Here there was far more contact between black and whites, trade unions were organizing confidently and there was a higher level of political discussion. The very day that Lumumba left prison he was taken by a white friend to different European bars, where he danced with Belgian women. The atmosphere in the capital was dramatically different from the rest of the country.

Belgium suffered much political turmoil after the war, with general questioning over the nature of the state. So in 1950 there was a national vote to see whether the royal family should be allowed to return, as King Léopold III was widely seen as having worked too closely with Germany during the war. When Léopold eventually took up residence in the Laeken Palace, he faced such a wave of protests that he was compelled to abdicate in favour of his son Baudouin.

Before long Lumumba made contact with the most important movers and shakers in the world of Léopoldville's politics. He met people who he had known before only by reputation. Many of these people were going to be caught up in the maelstrom of events leading up to independence. This included two important Josephs:

Ileo and Mobutu. The latter he met for the first time in the office of the newspaper *The Future* (*L'Avenir*). He made a strong impression on Lumumba; he spoke excellent French and soon became one of Lumumba's most loyal supporters. Mobutu admitted years later that he had fallen under the spell of Lumumba's idealism and was educated in 'Lumumba's school'.[88] The former, Ileo, became one of the founders of the *Mouvement National Congolais* (MNC) that would help lead the struggle to independence; he was also an important member of the *évolué* community in the capital. Lumumba immediately forced himself onto the political scene of the capital. Michel Djunga, a friend of Lumumba at the time recalled his sharp intelligence: 'he read a newspaper in a flash. He was informed on everything.'[89]

Lumumba's new job was with the brewery Bracongo, and it became a vital element in his political development. Established in Léopoldville since 1953 the brewery produced the beer Polar. Although Lumumba was first employed in the accounts department, within a year he had become the director in charge of promoting the beer. This was the first time a Congolese had occupied such a high position in the company. Competition between two beers divided the city. Primus – still drunk in the Congo today – was produced by Bralima. Lumumba received a salary of 25,000 francs, five times the salary he had earned in Stanleyville.

Despite being a teetotaler Lumumba was the perfect choice for the job. In his new position he used his talents of oratory to persuade people to switch from Primus to Polar. He rapidly learnt the language of the region, Lingala. But the work was vital in that it allowed him direct access to a wider public, and certainly communities far larger and more representative than the narrow world of *évolué* politics. As part of his new job he would visit bars in African neigbourhoods. Some of the largest and most important of these bars were the *Kongo-Bar* and the *Muyombe-Bar*. He even managed to create associations of drinkers dedicated to the promotion (and consumption) of the beer, *Amis Polar* (Friends of Polar) and *Papa Polar* for men and *Maman Polar* (Mother Polar) for female drinkers of the beer. Bars, beer and politics were the heady mix through which the idea of independence was spread in the capital. Lumumba made the most of the new job to spread his political creed, according to one account 'the publicity budget served as his political budget'.[90] This bar-politics – often expressed through the 'war of the beers' – of the late 1950s in Léopoldville was described by a white colleague of Lumumba's: 'The Belgian authorities never understood … that the true opinion of the indigenous masses were formed in the evenings in the bars of the *Cité* [African neighbourhoods] and not around tables at conferences in Brussels or Léopoldville.'[91]

Lumumba was elected president of the MNC on 10 October 1958, a party that sought a national reach and was going to become the instrument in which he would be elected Prime Minister in June 1960. But moves to create a national political movement predate Lumumba's arrival on the political scene in Léopoldville. Joseph Ileo, as early as August 1956, had attempted to build an organisation that was also to be called the *Mouvement National Congolais.* But the formation of political parties was still highly controlled. To form a political party the proposed leadership had to present itself to the authorities and nominate a white advisor. There was no tradition of political organisation.

In 1958 Belgian parliamentarians established a Working Group (*Groupe de Travail*) to gauge the aspirations and opinions of black and white people living in the Congo. The group represented both a change of thinking among certain people in Belgium – it was some sort of advance that the group was even constituted – and the absurdity of this exercise in 'consultation'. While the opinions of certain high-ranking whites in the colony were taken, there was no serious attempt to engage the Congolese. For many Congolese the group was a bitter joke. How could a group that did not have

Cyrille Adoula

any Congolese members be anything other than an insult? While it expressed the awakening in the metropolis towards a notion of political change in the Congo, the Working Group symbolised the continued arrogance of Brussels.

But it did have one beneficial effect: it radicalised opinion among the *évolués* and an increasingly militant urban population. On 26 August 1958, in the midst of the so-called 'consultation' and two days after General Charles de Gaulle made a speech in Brazzaville saying that he would offer independence to those under French rule in Africa, 16 prominent Congolese activists issued a petition praising the decision to decolonise the Congo but condemning the Working Group.

When the MNC was formed it pledged to fight against all forms of separatism and to obtain, 'within a reasonable' time and through negotiation, independence. Many of the main players of

Joseph Kasa Vubu

Congolese nationalism signed the declaration: Cyrille Adoula, Joseph Ileo and Patrice Lumumba. Cyrille Adoula had an interesting past; he was one of a few Congolese who had been able to complete his secondary education. He worked as a bank clerk and had recently helped to organise the first Congolese trade unions. Lumumba was elected president, Adoula and Gaston Diomi vice-presidents. But one notable absence was the signature of Joseph Kasa Vubu. He had refused to sign the petition in August and regarded the founding document of the MNC as far too moderate. His organisation ABAKO issued their own call for immediate independence one week after the foundation of the MNC, advocating the nationalisation of large companies.

Kasa Vubu, now middle-aged, had been a seminary student, and he shifted between forms of regionalist and national organisation. Sometimes he made radical statements calling for 'immediate independence', but frequently he appeared as a champion of regional identities. So for example in the 1940s, he had argued that the future ownership of the country should be in the hands of the Bakongo, those he regarded as descendants of the pre-colonial Kongo Empire, rather than the nation as a whole. For years ABAKO was seen much more narrowly as an organisation simply for the promotion of linguistic identity and a glorified social club.

Lumumba's election to president of the new organisation was a surprise to many. Although he was by far the most impressive member of the Congolese elite, he was relatively new to the city. By the end of October he was also elected to the leadership of the Batetela organisation. This meant that his only solid constituency was among the relatively small community of the Batetela in Léopoldville. But despite his relative obscurity Lumumba succeeded in imposing his character and vision on the MNC. When it came to the question of whether independence should be 'immediate' there were some important divisions. Kasa Vubu's call for independence (and his demand for nationalisation) was regarded by many of the ethnic affiliates of the MNC as far too radical. Lumumba did not necessarily share these reservations, but he did see the importance of holding the organisation and its potentially divisive membership together. If this meant that occasionally he had to hold his tongue, then so be it.

Pan-Africanism evolved as a response to European colonialism in Africa. Based on the belief that African people have a collective bond, pan-Africanism promotes the idea of continental unity. In the 20th century activists were increasingly attracted to pan-Africanism as the continent stretched towards independence. Some advocates of the philosophy believed that independence could not be complete until the entire continent was united. The movement for pan-African unity received its greatest boast when Ghana became independent in 1957. The country's first leader Kwame Nkrumah appointed a Pan-African Secretariat and held a series of international conferences from 1958 to 1961.

In April 1958 Kwame Nkrumah of Ghana had held the first African Conference of Independent African States in the capital of the newly independent state of Ghana in West Africa. Nkrumah made the decision that by the end of the year another conference, again in Accra, would be held but this time bringing together the political leaders of those states still under colonial tutelage. Lumumba and two other members of the MNC were invited to attend the conference. The event was titled the Sixth Pan-African Conference.

Lumumba obtained his passport, limiting him to attend in a 'personal capacity' and as a 'simple observer'. Like all serious political animals Lumumba ignored the visa stipulations and as representative of the MNC he made one of his most celebrated speeches at the Conference on 11 December. He began by speaking calmly about the situation in the Congo, informing those present about a colony many knew nothing about. Lumumba also spoke of the two-month old MDC that was fighting for a democratic and independent Congo. But when he turned his attention to the Conference he did not attempt to hold back:

Ghana was the model for many countries still under colonial control. The country had been independent since 1957, after years as a British colony. It was a paradoxical place. Many white people had stayed on to assist the new government. Even the Ghanaian army was run by British officers who were seconded to the Ghanaians until its own officers had been trained. At the same time the Prime Minister Kwame Nkrumah (1909–72) was an outspoken advocate for pan-Africanism. For a generation of young militants he was a figure to emulate. After December 1958 Nkrumah treated Lumumba, for better or worse, as his adopted son.

This historical conference which brings us in contact with qualified leaders of all the African countries and the entire world, reveals one thing to us: In spite of the frontiers that separate us, in spite of our ethnic difference, we have the same conscience, the same soul which bathes day and night in anguish, the same wish to make the African continent independent … free of uncertainty, fear of colonial domination.[92]

Lumumba met members of independent states and formed a close bond with the host president Nkrumah. He discussed tactics with delegates from the *Front Libération Nationale* of Algeria. The Congolese members also had meetings with Chinese and Soviet delegations, who expressed a keen interest in their struggle and offered their support in helping to rid the country of their colonial masters.

Africa was a continent of optimism. The conference in Accra reflected this hope. Although only a few countries on the continent had actually achieved independence by 1958, there was a firm sense that the continent was being buffeted by an irreversible wave of independence. This *liberating breath*, as Lumumba had put it in his address on 11 December, was felt in the conference halls in Accra, but also in every area of political life across the continent.[93] Africa was not the continent of troubled governance or 'wars' but of political liberation. Viewed from Accra nothing could stop the progress of African freedom and independence, and Africa seen from elsewhere in the world was perhaps the greatest hope for radical transformation. The buzz of political discussion, the exchange of strategy and tactics between members of different national liberation movements and the celebration of victories made the conference a place of intense expectation and excitement. Lumumba was transformed by the experience. The conference made a difference to his thinking, as Ludo de Witte explains 'It helped him to develop a Pan-African view which influenced his

The Soviet Union was an important symbol of development for the emerging independent nations in Africa. For anyone who had even a cursory knowledge of Soviet history they would have noted that the Soviet Union had been a semi-feudal state, peripheral to world development at the beginning of the century, but 50 years later it had emerged as a superpower to challenge the United States with growth rates to match Cold War rhetoric. Many Third World leaders saw lessons in the trajectory of the Soviet Union for developing their own new nations.

international perspective, the necessity of helping other liberation movements in Africa'.[94]

But these ideas were not entirely new to Lumumba. In his 1956 book he had declared that nationalism was a natural state *which binds the individual to the soil of his country, which inspire him to deeds of heroism for its defence … A man without any nationalist tendencies is a man without a soul.*[95]

Within days of his return from Ghana the first public meeting of the MNC was held on 28 December. The meeting was the first public baptism for the organisation, and it resounded with the radical energy of the Accra conference. Up to 3,000 people were said to attend, some saying that as many as 7,000 were present. Lumumba was no longer the grateful subject of the Belgian Congo: *Independence … must not be considered a present by Belgium, on the contrary … it is a right that the Congolese people have lost.*[96] If Kasa Vubu had been regarded as the radical voice of immediate independence then Lumumba soon overtook him.

Lumumba was consumed more than ever by political activity and had no time to sell beer. At the beginning of 1959 he resigned from his position at the brewery. Although only 18 months away from independence it is interesting to note that Lumumba was unique among the founding members of the MNC to do this. The others pursued their careers, making time in the evening and weekends for political mobilisation. Politics had been a hobby of the educated class; many wanted it to remain so. Perhaps Lumumba saw further than the others, Jacques Nijns, who knew Lumumba, argued that he 'lived only for political ideas, for the country and for the achievement of independence of the Congo.'[97]

Towards independence

The years 1959 and 1960 showed all the signs of radical upheaval: demonstrations; rioting and political discussion; a sense of expectation and hope and the collapse of old relationships. These changes were not limited to narrow circles of Congolese men who had been promoted by the colonial state. Tens of thousands of ordinary Congolese began to contemplate independence and freedom for the first time. These were the years of Congo's revolution.

One major event that helped to stimulate these upheavals was the rioting in Léopoldville on 4 January 1959. Officially 49 people were killed, but many Congolese put the number closer to 500. A legal demonstration had been called but the police intervened to disperse the crowd. This led to fighting between the authorities and the demonstrators, resulting in the destruction of symbols of European power: shops, cars and mission schools. In the aftermath of the riot the commanding officer of the *Force Publique*, General Emile Janssens, was unrepentant: 'We killed them because they were thieves, because they were pillagers … If they don't keep quiet, we are ready to recommence the sport'.[98] Europeans who had lived in the Congo – for years their private paradise – were overwhelmed with fear. The Congolese, for whom nothing would remain the same, determined to challenge colonial brutality. Europeans retreated further into their white enclaves; some even pressing for a military takeover of the colony. The Belgian government learnt the lesson; they must prepare for a rapid withdrawal from the Congo if they were to prevent further radicalisation.

The reaction of the MNC to the rioting was to send a telegram to the Belgian parliament demanding that they send a commission of enquiry to investigate the causes of the bloodshed. The rioting and the repression that followed actually left Lumumba and the MNC almost the only political force in Léopoldville. Kasa Vubu's ABAKO was dissolved by the authorities and its leading members arrested. But the MNC, though recently radicalised by the experience of the pan-African conference in Accra, still preached reconciliation, condemning both the repression *and* the rioting. In an interview in mid-January Lumumba expressed the MNC's firm commitment to total independence but with the understanding that a *period of transition* was necessary to prepare the Congolese for the heady tasks of government. He repeated what became a familiar refrain, that Europeans in the Congo had a vital role to play in the independence of the country. In arguing this Lumumba was repeating a position that he had held for several years. In 1956 he had written: *If the Congo should obtain its independence … why should you leave us and why should we drive you out … so long as we continue to treat each other … as true friends in the fullest meaning of the term.*[99]

The 1959 rebellion led to three important changes in Congolese society. Firstly, it saw the radicalisation of the Congolese population living in the capital, and triggered a wider involvement in the nationalist struggle. Secondly, it broke some of the conservative habits of the Congolese elite. Prior to the rebellion the attitude of the *évolués* centred on a determination to work within the colonial administration and win certain modest reforms for themselves. Suddenly another path opened up: the possibility of orientating a political programme towards the Congolese population. While the MNC might have continued to preach reconciliation and social peace, the effect of the rebellion on Lumumba was clear:

he was further radicalised. Lastly, the rebellion had a devastating effect on the Belgian royal family, as Ludo de Witte's explains: 'the Belgian royal family – which had a very strong ideological grip on all the colonialist structures – became scared. They realised that if Belgium wanted to hold onto the Congo, they had to respond to that radicalisation. A few days after the rebellion of Léopoldville the Belgian King was the first to mention the necessity of bringing a kind of independence to the Congo. And this declaration broke the spirit of all the hard-line colonists.'[100]

Perhaps for the first time the political scene shifted from the besuited, well-organised and respectable members of the *évolués* and their associations. Now the political centre of gravity could be found elsewhere, and not just in the capital. This lasted until 1960. In many rural areas the general questioning of colonial structures meant that villagers refused to pay taxes; new branches of ABAKO sprang up throughout Lower Congo; collections were made for those arrested on protests or for families who had lost loved ones. The entire colonial project that had been intact for generations unravelled. Hebert Weiss described the collapse of colonial authority. 'Suddenly people starting to express themselves with renewed confidence for the first time: Belgian-Congolese relations developed into a sort of game where the Congolese would "test" Belgian reactions with ambiguous attacks on authority, which if successful constituted a moral victory for the "assailant", but if resisted would prove difficult to punish or even to define in legal terms ... For instance, people refused to appear for the census, or mothers refused to appear with their children for medical examinations, or they asked that they be paid for bringing their children on the argument that the Belgians would not have insisted on doing this all these years if it did not bring them some advantage. Pregnant women also refused to be examined unless they received payment. There were also more subtle attacks on authority. People would no longer stand at attention when addressing administrators, they would be conspicuously slow in responding to questions put to them, and any incident would be immediately magnified. Thus a quarrel between a mission driver and a local villager, which would have been stopped previously by a stern word from a European nun, now would mushroom, and on occasion end with the pelting of the mission truck.'[101]

By the end of 1959 the colonial relationship of servant and master, that had seemed so solid a year before, had almost completely broken down. The same collapse was experienced across the country. At the end of October 1959 in Stanleyville the governor wrote in his journal:

'Sunday. Two incidents. Local games had been organised in front of a hotel in town for children irrespective of race. The atmosphere rapidly deteriorated, swarms of young black men destroyed the barriers that had been erected. It was necessary to stop the games. Frustrated, kids took out their anger on the furniture, breaking chairs, turning over tables. Another incident: a telephone call informed me that in the evening a European driver had hit a Congolese girl. Immediately the temperature rose. The police intervened, but they had to withdraw under a shower of stones and bottles. Finally, the gendarmerie stabilised the situation. Nine policemen have been injured.'[102]

Taxes were not paid; summonses to appear in the native courts were ignored; the local judges refused to work in their 'own' courts, and no notice was taken of colonial land regulations. For a time native authorities, so carefully developed and nurtured by the colonial government, melted into thin air.[103] What Lumumba had written from prison three years previously was much truer now: *The Congo is waking up. Her sons are emerging from their age-long sleep and trying to clear a way out into the light of day.*[104]

The MNC was not hegemonic on the political scene. Members left and new political formations were born. There were also political groups that had become more radical. Alphonse Nguvulu who had been one of the founding members of the MNC left the organisation in April 1959 to create with members of *Action Socialiste* the *Party of the People*, an explicitly socialist group. With the colonial authorities accepting the idea of independence Nguvulu was of the opinion that the MNC had already fulfilled its historical mission. The organisation should be dissolved and its members must join the ranks of the socialists, the only programme according to Nguvulu capable of leading the country to real independence and progress.

Pierre Mulele (1929–68) was born in a small village in the territory of Gungu in the Congo. Dismissed for being 'rebellious' from an apprenticeship in an Agriculture School in 1951, he was forced to join the army. Working in Léopoldville in 1953 he launched a campaign for the equal treatment of white and black civil servants. Mulele judged the MNC too moderate. After the rebellion in Léopoldville in 1959 he helped to establish the *Parti Solidaire Africain*, explaining: 'If we had at our disposal a good organisation and sufficient weapons we could have liberated the city'. Antoine Gizenga was also one of the first leaders of the PSA. After Lumumba's murder Mulele became the pre-eminent nationalist figure leading the fight against the pro-American government in the capital.

One of the more radical political parties to emerge was the *Parti Solidaire Africain*. Leading members of the PSA were Antoine Gizenga and Pierre Mulele. Similar to the MNC the PSA was led by members of the *évolués*. The National Central Committee and National Political Bureau in January 1960 were made up of teachers, bank or government clerks and medical assistants. But the party was changing. By early 1960 the party was beginning to base itself in the rural areas, among a completely different class of Congolese. These organisations, many explicitly socialist, exerted an important influence on the Congolese elite in the capital.

Building the party

On 13 January 1959 the Belgian King gave a national address responding to the riots. On the same day the conclusions of the

A moment of happiness as Patrice Lumumba becomes the first leader of an independent Congo in June 1960

farcical Working Group the previous year were announced. The report had been submitted to the new minister of the colonies Maurice van Hemelrijck in December. One conclusion was very significant; according to the report a large number of those consulted expressed a desire for 'internal autonomy'. The announcement explained that as a result Belgium would begin an 'exercise in universal suffrage'. Coached of course in words of dreadful condescension the report continued that the inhabitants of the Congo would in this way become capable of 'administering themselves'. To put this project in place Van Hemelrijck arrived in the Congo soon after the declaration. On 17 January he was received by a delegation of the MNC led by Lumumba. They expressed their agreement with the declaration of the Belgian government but only as a first step. The MNC wanted to see a Legislative Council emerge after proposed elections in December, when it would have real representatives of the people.

Lumumba rose on the tide of radicalism sweeping the country, by the end of March his tone changed again and he demanded from Belgium an exact date for independence. Lumumba told a reporter at the time that the MNC had 58,000 members. Even allowing for some exaggeration this is impressive for an organisation created less than five months previously. Matthais Kemishanga became a party organiser in Kasai very soon after he joined the MNC, and by the end of 1959 he was the provincial president in charge of propaganda. He describes the process of building the organisation: 'I joined the party in 1959, like everyone else I was a simple activist. But in June I was asked to help set up the party in Mweka and Luluabourg. I agreed. I took a train to the Mweka and days later we held a meeting. After the meeting we left for Luluabourg. In each place we passed we installed MNC committees, which would then organise the party in these areas.'[105]

Lumumba dedicated himself to spreading the message of the MNC around the country. His extraordinary energy meant that he could work 18 hours a day, exhausting his entourage and intimidating his rivals. On 28 March a permanent headquarters of the MNC was finally opened in the commune of Kinshasa. The HQ was also going to welcome all Congolese, whether members of the

MNC or not. Where everyone – no matter their specific political allegiance – could help build the movement, answer the telephone, write a letter or offer advice. Lumumba spoke everywhere he went, explaining the character of the anti-colonial struggle, demanding that the Belgian declaration was implemented immediately. Meetings multiplied and so did the numbers attending these meeting. The first congress of the MNC – which was also the first of any modern political party in the Congo – was held in Luluabourg (today's Kananga) in April.

Kemishanga was already an active member of the MNC. He arrived late to the congress: 'It was at the first congress of a political party in the Congo that I first saw Patrice Lumumba. When the congress had started I was not in Luluabourg, so I came in late. Lumumba was speaking. A journalist had just asked a question: "Monsieur Lumumba you ask for independence, but you don't have a single doctor, lawyer, geologist or a respected journalist. How are you going manage as an independent state?" Patrice Lumumba responded: "I am fully aware of this situation. But I have a question to ask you: You have been in the Congo for 80 years and you have not trained a single doctor or geologist. If we asked you to train ten doctors how many more years in our country will that take you?" The journalist was unable to respond.'[106]

Immediately after the congress Lumumba left for two trips, the first was to Conakry and then onto Belgium. Conakry was the capital of Guinea and the home to perhaps the most radical leader of independence at the time, Sékou Touré. His trip was important for the contacts he made with the Soviet Union. Lumumba's attitude to communism was informed largely by his ignorance on the subject: he had long rejected what he understood as class struggle which to him was an idea which would divide the Congo. Now, as he attempted to build unity across Congo's fractious political scene, this old position must have seemed even more pertinent.

Arriving in Brussels at the end of April Lumumba met Albert De Coninck, a member of the central committee of the Belgium Communist Party. De Coninck claimed that Lumumba was heavily influenced by his meetings with Sékou Touré, and under the president's influence he wanted to create a mass trade union movement in the Congo, to help him apply pressure on the colonial authorities. Lumumba promised to invite members of the Communist Party in Belgium to an MNC congress planned for June.

Sékou Touré (1922–84) was born in Faranah in central Guinea. In 1953 Touré became head of the Democratic Party of Guinea (*Parti Démocratique de Guinée*). When President Charles de Gaulle offered French colonies membership of a Franco-African community Touré was the only one to respond 'non', opting instead for immediate independence, famously commenting: 'We prefer poverty in freedom to riches in slavery'. Guinea gained independence in 1958. Guinea allied itself with the socialist bloc, and in 1965 broke off all relations with France.

Lumumba had decided that there were certain things to learn from the communists and much ideological baggage to discard. Although he was an increasingly intransigent nationalist leader, the pitch of his activism and declarations forever rising, he was still a pragmatist. Belgian colonial authority must be shown the door (and thrown through it if necessary), but Belgian technicians and experts must stay, although even this now came with a prefix: as long as they worked for the Congo's development and not its exploitation.

These trips were also extremely important for exploding myths about Belgium. Busselen describes the effect on Lumumba: 'It was important for Lumumba to see on his trip to Brussels that there were white men working as waiters, that there were prostitutes and that there was a white working class. He saw the reality of the so-called motherland. He could also access left-wing books for the first time.'[107] Lumumba's first trip to Belgium in 1956 had already changed his ideas about the Europeans: *I can assure you that quite a number of Congolese are in a much more comfortable situation than many Europeans in their home countries. We often have the mistaken idea that all Europeans live in the same conditions as the Europeans of the Congo, but this is a serious mistake.*[108]

Returning to the Congo in May Lumumba seems to have grown even less patient towards colonialism. Lumumba left for Stanleyville where he was going to establish a branch of the MNC. He was shocked by the conditions in the city since he had been arrested there three years previously. In May 1959 the city seemed particularly bereft of hope, without jobs and full of bitterness towards the colonial power. The city had in fact fallen into almost total lethargy, and the riots in the capital months before had only the faintest echo. No political pamphlet, declaration or act of solidarity with the demonstrators in Léopoldville is recorded. However among the city's European population there had been a shift: certain groups had started to hoard guns, others learnt how to shoot and appeals were made to the governor for stricter security measures.[109]

Lumumba was able to give voice to these grievances. After a few weeks in the city he became the conveyor belt for popular anger. But in Stanleyville the MNC also became the repository of social complaints. If the floodgates of colonial rule had burst open then many Congolese expressed this not only by automatically chanting independence but by complaining about low pay and unemployment and against their bullying, racist bosses. The MNC received a flow of letters

As colonial power began to crumble groups of Europeans organised themselves in European Volunteer Corps (*Corps de Voluntaires Européens*). They were armed patrols of white civilians, hated and feared by the Congolese. In reality these were vigilante groups who were allowed to police their neighbourhoods, parading in uniform and acting with impunity. As independence approached there were attempts to outlaw these groups. On 25 March 1960 civilians were forbidden from carrying arms and from patrolling the streets.

demanding action against 'vicious' employers and 'poor pay'. But the organisation was ill-prepared to respond to these demands, and instead they sought compromises with local companies and an 'understanding' between Europeans and the Congolese. After the riots in the capital the main trade union confederation the *Fédération Générale du Travail de Belgique* (FGTB) demanded a general increase in salaries. The MNC focused almost exclusively on independence and, was unable to satisfactorily develop a programme of social reforms.

Lumumba was acutely aware of the tensions that existed between the mass of popular support for the MNC and the leadership of the party who were often overly cautious. This relationship was dialectical: both the party and the movement grew and developed in the context of these tensions. In April 1959, while in Belgium, Lumumba responded to a question about support for the party among the Congolese masses: *the masses are a lot more revolutionary than us … They do not always dare to express themselves in front of a police officer, or make their demands in front of an administrator but when we are with them it is the masses who push us, and who want to move more rapidly than us.*[110]

Lumumba's work in Stanleyville also involved fundraising. Money raised in the city was used to buy bicycles, vehicles and to fund propagandists who worked recruiting members to the MNC in rural areas. These party militants were overwhelmingly young, and soon developed radical slogans drawn from their experiences during the recruitment drive. Young organisers also filled in the gaps in the campaign, making promises to the villagers that became part of the MNC programme, even if the leadership of the party were reluctant: the end to the forced cultivation of cotton, a suspension of taxes and an end to police abuses. Weis argued that these tensions characterised the development of political parties in the Congo, 'the rural masses tended to be radical and the leaders frequently tried to dampen these predilections on the part of their followers.'[111]

Nationalism, independence and class

The inability of the MNC to adequately give voice to the complaints that came from workers, trade unionist and those who sought an outlet for their economic and social demands, reveals a problem with the politics of independence. The MNC – with Lumumba at its centre – could only reply with the battle-cry 'immediate independence'. The party did not have the political vocabulary to construct a programme of social transformation that could envisage more than 'independence'.

Even though the demand for independence was a radical slogan it contained many contradictions. Lumumba was the figurehead of this radicalising movement and saw a new state powering development in an independent Congo, with, if possible, Belgian and foreign assistance. Essentially the struggle was a democratic one; it sought elections to a new state, but the Congolese would remain employees in mostly foreign-owned companies, in a country whose very creation was an extremely recent colonial invention.

Consistent with national liberation movements across the continent at the time the objective was not to fundamentally upset the *status quo*. The world was divided into nations, and the struggle for national liberation was an attempt to establish an independent territory for capitalist or – in the cases of those states looking to the Soviet Union – state capitalist development. In this context all national classes had to unite as the project of liberation insisted on unity.

Lumumba's ideas fitted perfectly into these holes. For several years he had shunned any notion of 'class struggle', which was to him a metropolitan idea imported from Belgium. In 1956 he wrote: *Let poor Belgium keep its ideological squabbles. The Congo needs something other than petty wranglings. Let us all unite, Catholics, Liberals, Socialist, Christians, Protestants, Atheists, to achieve real peace in this country.* On socialist ideas he was dismissive: *Our country has much greater need of 'builders' than of squabblers, pamphleteers and purveyors of communist slogans.*[112] His position on many things changed, but on these questions it did not: an independent Congo must remain united. One easy way of arguing for unity in a society divided by class, was to deny the very existence of classes. For Lumumba – in his rhetoric at least – the class struggle simply did not exist.

Frantz Fanon (1925–1961) was born on the Caribbean island of Martinique. He moved to Algeria to work as a doctor in 1953, just before the start of the war for independence. He became the foremost thinker and activist of national liberation. *The Wretched of the Earth* is Fanon's most famous work. In the book he describes the experience of national liberation and noted how Cuba, which gained independence in 1902, remained entirely dependent on the US. He was scathing about the 'African bourgeoisie' who had led their countries to independence; they have 'learnt nothing from books. If they had looked closer at the Latin American countries they doubtless would have recognised the dangers which threaten them.'

There was no serious attempt to organise among trade unionist, or to build a political project on the ability of workers and the 'rural masses' to destabilise the colonial economy, through strikes and occupations. The resting place for the independence struggle was in the nation state, which occupied a space in a fiercely competitive world system. This much Lumumba knew. He understood that the real battle to build up the Congolese state would come after independence; in preparation he explained that the Congolese would have to *tighten their belts*. Lumumba was beating a familiar drum: *Tomorrow, it is work … We must redouble our efforts. We must drink one bottle of beer in place of two … We must mobilise ourselves to create a national economy.*[113]

Other nationalist leaders had discovered that once independence had been won old repressive and colonial structures would have to be used to maintain the fiction of class unity. Lumumba's contemporary Frantz Fanon could see the dangers inherent in the African national liberation struggle. He explained how the national bourgeoisie – the Congolese *évolué* – degenerates after independence into the exploiting class that they had supplanted. He wrote how the class of nationalist leaders becomes 'a sort of little caste, avid and voracious ... only too glad to accept the dividends that the former colonial power hands out to it.'[114]

The struggle for economic growth, and the accumulation of mining capital in the Congo, would force the new elite into an exploitative relationship to the poor and working class as the only way of powering development. In the new nations emerging on the continent, this is exactly what happened. Colonial oppression of the poor continued after independence under the fiction of class harmony, or for those so-called radical states, 'African socialism'. The result was as John Molyneux explained: 'the seemingly radical, fluid structures of the nationalist revolution settle into the Stalinist mould of the bureaucratic one-party state'.[114]

Fanon, observing at close hand the struggle for Algerian freedom, described the process that transformed national liberation into 'the curse of independence, and the colonial power through its immense resources of coercion condemns the young nation to regression. In plain words, the colonial power says: "Since you want independence, take it and starve."'[116] The Congo was caught in this vice; between a cowardly *évolué* and the limitations of national development in the post-colonial world.

The MNC splits

Lumumba was used to being the target of envy and jealousy. There were serious rumblings in his own party; he was accused of vanity, 'congenital narcissism' and mad personal ambitions. Joseph Ileo, a co-founder of the MNC, began to orchestrate Lumumba's removal for crimes of 'vanity'. Ileo led a split in July 1959, which was described as the revocation of Lumumba's presidency. He took with him most of the leading members of the organisation. But it was a split without any popular backing. The membership stayed

Albert Kalonji

with Lumumba. Lumumba did not waste anytime and he sought to build the MNC which now came with the postfix 'Lumumba'.

The two factions both calling themselves the MNC organised separately, recruited members and held separate congresses. In October congresses were held by the two factions almost simultaneously, Lumumba's in Stanleyville and Ileo's in Elisabethville. Albert Kalonji, recently released from prison, briefly tried to reconcile Lumumba with the group assembling in Katanga. Kalonji was an important player in Congolese politics. He had been born in 1929 and educated in a Catholic mission and then trained and worked as an agricultural assistant for the colonial state. He became involved in the journal *Présence Africaine*, and in the late 1950s attended 'cultural and political' events in Brussels and Paris. As a founding member of the MNC with Lumumba he spoke from the left, condemning colonialism in increasingly hysterical tones and declaring that the USSR would come to the aid of the Congo. In August 1959 he was arrested for inciting a strike and having distributed a 'seditious' publication. Having failed to reconcile Lumumba and Ileo he turned up in Elisabethville and was elected president of the MNC. But the MNC-Kalonji was an empty shell: in Léopoldville its base had more or less disintegrated. Its leading figures, Ileo and Adoula had done nothing to build the organisation.

As president of the rival faction of the MNC Kalonji started to organise in the Kasai among the Baluba. The abandonment of once-loyal comrades must have induced a certain dizziness in Lumumba. Lumumba understood what these splits really meant, writing in January 1960 *Me, I advocate UNITY, the Kalonji … and Ileo advocate DIVISION. From the moment of its formation in October 1958, the MNC opted for unity. At the conference held in April 1959 with different political parties in Luluabourg, we affirmed this position … The entire doctrine of the MNC is based on the unity of the Congo.*[117]

For most members of the *évolué* political parties were seen as a method for controlling resources and accessing wealth. With the first disagreement people left and formed new organisations. Even Lumumba, who was a leader with an impressive ability to mobilise and to speak, had only started to build a political party. Busselen

Ethnic divisions in the Congo were constantly being manipulated by colonial authorities. The division between the Baluba and the Bena Lulua was not some ancient tribal animosity, but the result of European patronage. Europeans of *Forminière*, the diamond mines, favoured the Baluba, identifying them as excellent workers. But Bena Lulua were denied similar opportunities. Despite the fact that both groups had emerged out the same community they started to see each other as competitors in the allocation of land and jobs. As the Congo moved towards independence political parties in the Congo organised themselves along these ethnic cleavages. So CONAKAT became the main party of the Lunda and BALUBAKAT represented many members of the Buluba community in Katanga.

argues that: 'most of the political class was minor clerks and intellectuals eager to mimic the white man. They could see that the colonists were leaving and they wanted to take their place. Parties were identified as the tool for securing positions in a new state. The tragedy for Lumumba was that he had no real organisational structure to defend him in 1960.'[118]

Lumumba's second arrest

Promises issued by the Belgian government at the beginning of 1959 had come to nothing. Lumumba was not alone in doubting the promises of the Belgians; it became clear to him through the course of 1959 that only struggle could free the Congolese. He declared that the MNC would boycott the elections planned for December. The MNC would have to steel itself to organise the fight for independence. Lumumba saw himself and the ideas he espoused in the context of the continent's radical movements for liberation. In the first issue of the new newspaper of the MNC *Indépendance* the pictures of Lumumba, Sekou Touré, Nkrumah and Kasa Vubu were printed to demonstrate this continuity. Lumumba was developing his politics and organisation in a pan-Africanist mould.

To organise the party further the MNC resolved to hold a congress in Stanleyville in October. Lumumba's address at the closing rally displayed his growing impatience and anger: *Dear brothers no collaboration is any longer possible with Belgium … Dear Brothers we do not pursue any personal ambitions … If we had wanted money … we would not be doing what we are doing today. And now my brothers we are asked to vote in December! But for your oppressed brother, who suffers, who wants immediate independence do not vote! … All our women, all our children, the strength of the country, all our energies, we mobilise them in the service of the Congolese revolution. The Belgians have decided! They have established two military bases, one in Kamina and the other in Kitona … why all these bases, it is to intimidate us … Belgium will kill us ... And that will be in the name of religion and of the civilisation that they have bought us.*[119]

Shortly after the closure of the conference on 30 October Stanleyville erupted in rioting. Dozens were seriously injured and 26 killed. These events were not entirely linked Stanleyville suffered from serious unemployment and growing anti-colonial sentiment, but the MNC had given this discontent political direction. Lumumba was arrested, accused of having 'worked-up' the population into a frenzy of anger and disobedience. The governor Pierre Leroy accused Lumumba of 'haranguing' the population of the city on a daily basis. An arrest warrant went out for Lumumba on 30 October; he hid for two days before being found.

Round Tables

As early as 1956 Lumumba had envisaged some sort of commission made up of Congolese and Belgian officials to discuss the possible autonomy of the Congo. But now in very different circumstances a similar idea began to emerge. In Elisabethville the MNC-Kalonji made the demand of a Round Table discussion on the future of the Congo. ABAKO and the PSA took up the slogan. The new minister of the colonies August de Schryver announced that a 'round table' conference would indeed take place but only after the elections in December.

The elections were a source of considerable controversy. Most parties opposed them; the MNC-Lumumba had also decided to boycott them. Lumumba believed that they were sham elections to colonial institutions that would only serve to reinforce the colonial state. But in November the MNC reversed their earlier decision to boycott. The MNC did extremely well, in Stanleyville the party won 80 per cent of the vote. But the results were uneven. In the areas where the party – and Lumumba in particular – had made little effort to build they scored abysmally.

The party's electoral triumph in December was followed in

January by a sentence of six months imprisonment for its president. But calls for Lumumba's release became deafening, from both those Congolese politicians assembling in Brussels for the Round Table Conference and from Belgian politicians and ministers. He was transferred to Katanga on 22 January, arriving in the capital Elisabethville onboard an aircraft belonging to Sabena. He was photographed emerging from the plane, with a slightly dazed expression, barefooted and still in his filthy prison clothes. He was then transferred to the prison in Jadotville and eventually flown to Brussels on 26 January, bruised and blooded from his ordeal. Lumumba spoke of his liberation from prison two weeks afterwards: *I was thrown on the plane. My neck was twisted. I have been manhandled; all my things are still in prison. I arrived in Elisabethville leaving the plane like a criminal, where some Europeans amused themselves by photographing me.*[120]

He was greeted by supporters at the airport in Brussels. Mobutu was there, as well as Kalonji. But perhaps the most memorable well-wisher was an old Belgian woman who had stood patiently waiting with a bunch of flowers. When she saw Lumumba she rushed up to him and forced the bouquet into his arms and kissed him with the words, 'I am only one poor woman but there are millions of others like myself. In their name I want to salute a freedom fighter.'[121]

The Round Table Conference opened on 20 January 1960 in Brussels. Every delegation had been allocated a Belgian advisor, to guide the delegation through the discussions: only the MNC-L opted for a Congolese one. When Lumumba arrived the atmosphere was electrified. Within days of his release the date of 30 June 1960 was agreed for independence. The Belgian state had been forced to concede immediate independence: the battle cry from the street. It is worth pausing here to note how remarkable this was: four years beforehand the government had envisaged a 30-year plan towards independence, which had shrunk dramatically to five years in 1959 and then six months in January 1960. This was, by any account, an extraordinary change. But there were challenges; the country had fewer than 30 African university graduates in the entire territory, and only three out of some 5,000 management-level positions in the civil service filled by Congolese. Where were the Congolese technicians and bureaucrats who could run the new state? The MNC-L insisted on a rapid programme of training for the Congolese provided by Belgium.

After the date for independence had been agreed substantive issues were discussed. The main debate centred on those who supported federalism and those defending a unitary state. Lumumba insisted on a centralised state, with its capital in Léopoldville and that Belgium should not be allowed to define the future structures of independence. He seemed already worried about the possibility of Belgium dividing up the state before independence had even been won.

But the discussion on federalism revealed another more serious agenda. The main issue was Katanga whose Congolese representatives had indicated that they wanted autonomy. Katanga was the powerhouse of the Congolese economy, contributing more than two-thirds of the national income. The leading political figure in Katanga was Moise Tshombe. *Observer* journalist Colin Legum described him in the following terms: 'Tshombe, the 42-year-old leader of the *Conféderation des Associations Tribales du Katanga* (CONAKAT) was never part of the nationalist movement. In the days of colonialism he stuck close to the Belgians, and had he been as good a businessman as his father (who left him a string of businesses) he would have prospered. But he lost his patrimony and went bankrupt three times. However he never stayed down for long. Like many unsuccessful businessmen he became a leading figure in the politics of commerce: he was President of the African Chamber of Commerce Association.'[122]

Tshombe and Lumumba clashed during the Round Table

discussions. Lumumba feared that federalism for Tshombe was a cloak concealing his ambitions to head an independent Katanga at the service of foreign powers. Tshombe insisted that all mineral wealth should remain the property of provincial states and should be controlled (and presumably distributed) by them. Lumumba asked: *What is the purpose of independence, if tomorrow the Congo is ripped apart by us?*[123] Again Lumumba won the day. Katanga belonged to the Congo and the wealth of that province would be controlled by the national state. Lumumba was already clear that Tshombe's federalism was a disguise for separatism. When Tshombe returned to the Congo he dismissed the conference as 'useless'.

However, there were important outstanding issues. The Belgian government argued the question of the two military bases recently established in Kamina and Kitona and the exact role of the *Force Publique* would only be resolved after independence. Despite the arguments the mood at the conference was positive. Lumumba was still hopeful about a smooth transition to independence which would see the cooperation of the Belgian government. Legum reported from the conference, 'When I talked to Lumumba at the Round Table Conference in Brussels in January 1960, he was still eloquently optimistic about his relations with the Belgians, despite his recent imprisonment and ill-treatment as a prisoner.'[124]

Lumumba returned to Léopoldville at the end of February with one clear victory already. The Round Table Conference had gone his way. Now his main task was to organise for the elections in May. The Belgians started their campaign against Lumumba. Between May and June, the Belgian authorities were determined to supervise the elections themselves. Directly influencing the national press to warn of Lumumba's alleged communism, they financed rival politicians to ensure that only compliant parties would get elected. Those political organisations that based themselves on ethnic and regional fiefdoms secured funding from Belgium. These loyal ethnic-based parties reflected the pattern of colonial rule since the late 19th century. For Brussels these parties were the best chance after 1960 for maintaining the Congo as an acquiescent and dependent state. In many cases Brussels' strategy worked; in Katanga for example, from a total of 325 rural council seats, 276 seats were captured by ethnic or local candidates.[125] But the MNC won through. On the national stage the MNC secured 33 seats, by far the largest number of seats for a single party. On 23 June the first nationally elected government of the Congo was established, with Lumumba's allies taking a clear majority in the 137-member national assembly.[126]

However, Lumumba was compelled to distribute power to his rivals, including Joseph Kasa Vubu, who became the first president. The result was a coalition government. With independence only days away the economic outlook was bleak: 'On the eve of its independence the Government was faced with large current deficits … The flight of capital and the loss of international confidence, because of the events of 1959, meant the new Government would come to power with no liquid assets at all.'[127] Lumumba urged his supporters to prepare themselves for a long period of hard work. Although Lumumba had seen to what extent Belgium was prepared to interfere in a post-independent Congo, he could have had no idea of the lengths to which they would to go to ensure that the country remained under their control.

Political elimination

The decision to eliminate Lumumba was made long before his physical elimination in January 1961. It was the explicit, if secret, policy of the Belgian government after the Round Table Conference. Lumumba had aroused the disgust of the Belgian government, colonial administrators and the Europeans still residing in the Congo. But what had he done to earn such enmity?

For more than a year before the conference he had become the militant and tireless organiser for the MNC. Moving around the

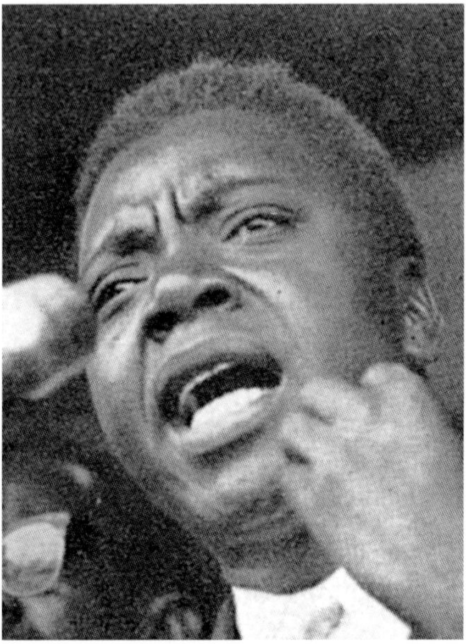

Moise Tshombe

country Lumumba argued for independence and quickly became strident in his condemnation of colonialism. He no longer proclaimed a 'Belgian-Congolese' community or praised the work of colonialism. But his radicalism, so often misunderstood, did not come about from some sudden conversion to communism. Although Lumumba had contact with Soviet embassy officials on his travels, he was no more a communist than the leader of CONAKAT, Moise Tshombe. Part of this radicalism came about from his experience of imprisonment in 1956–7; he suffered more from the abuses of colonialism than any other member of the *évolué*. However most of all he was transformed by events in the Congo after his release, and by a growing rejection of the colonial project by workers, the unemployed and the rural poor. Lumumba became the conduit for these popular demands.

Lumumba had become the embodiment of the movement

for independence. His daughter Juliana comments: 'my father's political life lasted just three years, he developed with incredible speed. Everything that he finally demanded, "immediate independence" he was not the first to demand but he became the incarnation of independence; he became the representative and the symbol for immediate independence.'[128] During Congo's revolution time became a remarkably fluid concept. Lumumba was inspired by a movement that was developing rapidly around him, and he helped provided it with a voice, slogans and the first outlines of an organisation. His son François Lumumba describes how his father 'entered the consciousness of the Congolese and added an irrepressible dynamism to independence'.[129]

Belgium's decision to grant independence so quickly was connected to this political change. Ludo de Witte argues that they 'saw that there was a process of political change in 1959, and they wanted to move quicker than this radicalisation hoping that at the time of the election – and this was the opinion of the Belgian ruling elite – that 80 per cent of the Congolese parliament would be filled with docile pro-Belgian MPs while only 20 per cent would be radicals. But they miscalculated the extent of the radicalisation.'[130] The objective of granting independence to curtail radical political change was common in many African countries during this period. In most instances the strategy succeeded, but in the Congo it failed.

When Lumumba finally arrived at the Round Table Conference, bandaged from his brutal treatment in Elisabethville, he dominated his Congolese colleagues but also the European politicians who still regarded themselves as his natural superiors. He was uncompromising and refused to allow Belgium to retain any powers after independence, rejecting the absurd notion that the Belgian King could become the head of state in an independent Congo. He also ridiculed Tshombe's notion that provincial wealth should be controlled by the provinces alone. He aroused the jealousy of his

Congolese counterparts but also the anger of Belgian politicians. Even in the dying hours of colonialism the Belgian government remained unapologetic. To them Lumumba was still a loquacious native who obstinately refused to accept his place.

When Lumumba returned to the Congo after the conference the idea of his political elimination was already being hatched by Brussels. But their hands had been tied. Lumumba had emerged internationally as the pre-eminent leader of Congolese independence. Another strategy had to be prepared. From now on they sought to make alliances against Lumumba, with what they regarded as moderate forces antagonistic to the MNC-L.

A plan was drawn up between Harold d'Aspremont-Lynden, Minister for African Affairs for the Prime Minster Gaston Eyskens, and the advisor on African affairs Professor Arthur Doucy on 1 March 1960. The first point of this plan was the choice of advisors who would direct the Congo before and after independence, but point three was the most important, it concerned the elimination of Lumumba by organising political forces opposed to him:

> 3. Political Action: Man to eliminate is Lumumba … regroup moderate forces by province … : Katanga: Conakat … Kasai: Kalonji … It would be necessary to make available to these parties technicians, propaganda and funds. The total could cost a maximum of 50 millions …[131]

Point Four concerned the choice of a reliable Congolese ally for the Belgians. But for the moment Brussels failed.

Independence: 30 June 1960

Congolese independence was declared on 30 June 1960, and celebrations across the country lasted for days. The Independence Day ceremony was held in the presence of King Baudouin of Belgium who patronisingly sought to grant the Congo freedom in the name of the Belgian state. The day did not turn out as anyone predicted. Officially the event was due to take place in the parliament building in front of the Belgian elite, newly-elected members of the Congolese parliament and foreign dignitaries and reporters. Like many such ceremonies at the time, it was seen simply as the official announcement of a negotiated independence, involving speeches, handshakes and the lowering and raising of flags. The *Guardian* reported on 1 July, 'The crowd around the wide square of the *Palais des Nations* was as small, and as unenthusiastic as an independence crowd could be. There were only about 4,000 there, due, perhaps, to the confusion caused by hasty arrangements. But the shouts of *"Le Roi"* from loyal Belgians as the King entered the Parliament Building was the first cheering note for him.'[132]

Lumumba's wife, Pauline, refused to attend the ceremony. Their daughter, Juliana, explains: 'In the morning before the ceremony they had an argument. As my father was leaving the house for the palace, my mother started to throw his things off the balcony. That's my mother, she has a terrible temper'.[133]

Lumumba had not been scheduled to speak, and the government was to be represented by its President, Joseph Kasa Vubu.

The King rose to announce the official end of Belgian rule in the Congo, but he did much more. His speech turned into a historical justification for the crimes of colonisation, he argued that the last 80 years had seen development and the fulfilling of the white man's burden. The King pronounced: 'The independence of the Congo is the crowning glory of the work conceived by the genius of King Léopold II, undertaken by him with firm courage, and continued by Belgium with perseverance. Independence marks a decisive hour in the destinies not only of the Congo herself but – dare I say – of the whole of Africa. For eighty years Belgium has sent to your land the best of her sons, first to deliver the Congo basin from the odious slave trade which was decimating her population, later to bring together the different tribes which, though former enemies, are now preparing to form the greatest of the independent states of Africa. [These] pioneers deserve admiration from us and acknowledgement from you. They built communications, founded a medical service, modernised agriculture, and built cities and industries and schools.' To compound the insult, King Baudouin continued, 'It is now up to you, gentlemen, to show that you are worthy of our confidence.'[134]

When the King finished there was a respectful round of applause before Kasa Vubu replied, acknowledging the 'wisdom' of the Belgium state. Lumumba followed, fully aware of the significance of the event. Lumumba sorted the pages of his speech that he had hastily prepared the night before:

Men and women of the Congo,

Victorious fighters for independence, today victorious, I greet you in the name of the Congolese Government. All of you, my friends, who have fought tirelessly at our sides, I ask you to make this June 30, 1960, an illustrious date that you will keep indelibly engraved in your hearts, a date of significance of which you will teach to your children, so that they will make known to their sons and to their grandchildren the glorious history of our fight for liberty.

For this independence of the Congo, even as it is celebrated today with Belgium, a friendly country with whom we deal as equal to equal, no Congolese worthy of the name will ever be able to forget that is was by fighting that it has been won {applause}, a day-to-day fight, an ardent and idealistic fight, a fight in which we were spared neither privation nor suffering, and for which we gave our strength and our blood.

We are proud of this struggle, of tears, of fire, and of blood, to the depths of our being, for it was a noble and just struggle, and indispensable to put an end to the humiliating slavery which was imposed upon us by force.

This was our fate for eighty years of a colonial regime; our wounds are too fresh and too painful still for us to drive them from our memory. We have known harassing work, exacted in exchange for salaries which did not permit us to eat enough to drive away hunger, or to clothe ourselves, or to house ourselves decently, or to raise our children as creatures dear to us.

We have known ironies, insults, blows that we endured morning, noon, and evening, because we are Negroes. Who will forget that to a black one said 'tu', certainly not as to a friend, but because the more honorable 'vous' was reserved for whites alone?

We have seen our lands seized in the name of allegedly legal laws which in fact recognized only that might is right.

We have seen that the law was not the same for a white and for a black, accommodating for the first, cruel and inhuman for the other.

We have witnessed atrocious sufferings of those condemned for their political opinions or religious beliefs; exiled in their own country, their fate truly worse than death itself.

We have seen that in the towns there were magnificent houses for the whites and crumbling shanties for the blacks, that a black was not admitted in the motion-picture houses, in the restaurants, in the stores of the Europeans; that a black travelled in the holds, at the feet of the whites in their luxury cabins.

Who will ever forget the massacres where so many of our brothers perished, the cells into which those who refused to submit to a regime of oppression and exploitation were thrown?

All that, my brothers, we have endured.

But we, whom the vote of your elected representatives have given the right to direct our dear country, we who have suffered in our body and in our heart from colonial oppression, we tell you very loud, all that is henceforth ended.

The Republic of the Congo has been proclaimed, and our country is now in the hands of its own children.

Together, my brothers, my sisters, we are going to begin a new struggle, a sublime struggle, which will lead our country to peace, prosperity, and greatness.

Together, we are going to establish social justice and make sure everyone has just remuneration for his labour {applause}.

We are going to show the world what the black man can do when he works in freedom, and we are going to make of the Congo the centre of the sun's radiance for all of Africa.

We are going to keep watch over the lands of our country so that they truly profit her children. We are going to restore ancient laws and make new ones which will be just and noble.

We are going to put an end to suppression of free thought and see to it that all our citizens enjoy to the full the fundamental liberties foreseen in the Declaration of the Rights of Man.

We are going to do away with all discrimination of every variety and assure for each and all the position to which human dignity, work, and dedication entitles him.

We are going to rule not by the peace of guns and bayonets but by a peace of the heart and the will.

And for all that, dear fellow countrymen, be sure that we will count not only on our enormous strength and immense riches but on the assistance of numerous foreign countries whose collaboration we will accept if it is offered freely and with no attempt to impose on us an alien culture of no matter what nature {applause}.

In this domain, Belgium, at last accepting the flow of history, has not tried to oppose our independence and is ready to give us their aid and their friendship, and a treaty has just been signed between our two countries, equal and independent. On our side, while we stay vigilant, we shall respect our obligations, given freely.

Thus, in the interior and the exterior, the new Congo, our dear Republic that my government will create, will be a rich, free, and prosperous country. But so that we will reach this aim without delay, I ask all of you, legislators and citizens, to help me with all your strength.

I ask all of you to forget your tribal quarrels. They exhaust us. They risk making us despised abroad.

I ask the parliamentary minority to help my Government through a constructive opposition and to limit themselves strictly to legal and democratic channels.

I ask all of you not to shrink before any sacrifice in order to achieve the success of our huge undertaking.

In conclusion, I ask you unconditionally to respect the life and the property of your fellow citizens and of foreigners living in our country. If the conduct of these foreigners leaves something to be desired, our justice will be prompt in expelling them from the territory of the Republic; if, on the contrary, their conduct is good, they must be left in peace, for they also are working for our country's prosperity.

The Congo's independence marks a decisive step towards the liberation of the entire African continent.

Sire, Excellencies, Mesdames, Messieurs, my dear fellow

countrymen, my brothers of race, my brothers of struggle – this is what I wanted to tell you in the name of the Government on this magnificent day of our complete independence.

Our government, strong, national, popular, will be the health of our country.

I call on all Congolese citizens, men, women and children, to set themselves resolutely to the task of creating a prosperous national economy which will assure our economic independence.

Glory to the fighters for national liberation!

Long live independence and African unity!

Long live the independent and sovereign Congo![135]

Lumumba finally finished the speech – to 'loud and long' applause – and returned to his chair. The programme was interrupted for an hour as the King threatened to leave. The King, as the personification of Belgian power, had correctly taken the speech as a personal insult. This was an insult that the Belgian establishment would never forgive. The Belgian press called for revenge. Never had the dignity of the Belgian state been so insulted. Even Benoît Verhaegem, the acclaimed academic of the Congo, declared that the speech was an 'unpardonable error.'[136]

For those who opposed colonialism, the day had been a triumph. In New York, Malcolm X told his followers that Lumumba's independence-day speech was the 'greatest speech', and that it had been made by the 'greatest black man who ever walked the African continent.'[137] Lumumba had turned 30 June 1960 into a day of victory, showing to the world how independence in the Congo was really won.

Independence was not simply a day of official celebrations in the capital, attended by foreign dignitaries and Congolese politicians. It was a moment of national rejoicing that expressed exactly the popular struggle for independence that Lumumba had spoken about in his speech. Asse Lilombo was 13 years old and lived in

A prime ministerial wave from Patrice Lumumba

the Province of Léopoldville: 'It was a big feast, a party of liberation. We had been liberated from slavery. The women were dressed up. There was goat and beer. The party lasted days. It was not only a party of independence; it was a party of liberation. We would be responsible for ourselves. We would manage our country ourselves.'[138] Mbara Emmanual Bastin was in a Protestant mission school at the time of independence. Since 1959 he had been known by his family as 'Emery' after Lumumba. Bastin remembers a moment of extraordinary celebration: 'a procession of the students from local primary schools was organised, one from the protestant school, and another from the Catholic one. Then there were the games ... Everyone knew that we were leaving a state of slavery. Everywhere enormous demonstrations were organised to mark the passage to independence and everywhere we heard the name of Lumumba: Lumumba the "father of Independence". When Patrice Lumumba spoke the radio vibrated right into the heart of the country. You put the radio on the table and it vibrated as if his voice had an extraordinary power.'[139]

Political parities, class and ethnicity

Patrice Lumumba was the first prime minister of independent Congo. The MNC, though not explicitly radical in its programme of reform, was pledged to create a unitary, multi-ethnic state, which would promote the redistribution of wealth to the poor. The other major players on the political scene were ABAKO, led by Joseph Kasa Vubu, CONAKAT run by the rich middle-class *évolué* Moise Tshombe, which hoped to see the Bena Lulua dominate Katanga either in a federal Congo or, if necessary, as a separate state and Balubakat, also in Katanga, was led by Jason Sendwe. Balubakat were suspicious of CONAKAT and the Bena Lulua, and meant that Tshombe could not speak unanimously for Katanga.

The process of independence in the Congo in 1960, but also across the continent, was simply one that saw the *deracialisation* of the colonial state. Citizenship ceased to rest on a racial membership. But this left the system of rural governance almost entirely unreformed, and consequently ethnic divisions firmly entrenched. It was these ethnic divisions that dominated the political scene in the Congo in the months after independence.

While the Congo was moving towards independence, there were many people trying to frustrate it. One observer was reported in the Belgian newspaper *La Releve*, 'Independence was never intended to be anything but "purely fictitious and nominal". Financial circles believed, our political circles were more naïve than anything, that it would be enough to give a few Congolese leaders the title of "Minister" or "Deputy" with decorations, luxury motor-cars, big salaries and splendid houses in the European quarter, in order to put a definite stop to the emancipation movement which threatened the financial interests concerned.'[140]

The Belgian economy was intimately connected to its colonial possession in central Africa; the country had extensive public and private investment in the Congo while at least a third of Belgium's trade was imports from Africa. By the end of the 1950s, the *Union Minière* earned an annual profit of 4 billion Belgian francs. After Tshombe's declaration of independence for Katanga, *Union Minière* had enough petty cash to deposit 1.25 billion francs into his bank account. The Congo cornered another mineral market: cobalt mining in the late 1950s represented three quarters of global production. For those Belgian companies with a large stake in the Congo, there was no talk of leaving the country without a struggle.[141]

The struggle for real independence

Within days of Lumumba's speech, the first of the mutinies of the *Force Publique* took place. The soldiers had hoped independence would actually mean something, that it would improve their pay and their rank. When these changes did not happen, they took the decision to kick out some of their white officers themselves. There was violence. One of the triggers for the mutinies was a speech made by General Emile Janssens to his soldiers on 5 July, explaining to them the true nature of independence: 'As I have always told you order and discipline will be maintained as they have always been. Independence brings changes to politicians and to civilians. But for you, nothing will be changed. ... None of your new masters can change the structure of an army which, throughout its history, has been the most organised, the most victorious in Africa. The politicians have lied to you.'[142]

After delivering this sermon he proceeded to write on a blackboard facing the assembled men: 'Before independence = after independence'. All hell broke loose. Later in the day soldiers began to demand that Janssens must go, to be replaced by a Congolese commander. They started to riot. Lumumba summoned Janssens, who tried to insist that Belgian soldiers should be brought in from bases in Kamina and Kitona to teach the rebels a lesson. Lumumba refused. He did the opposite and immediately gave each soldier a promotion in rank. On 6 July he dismissed Janssens. The old name *Force Publique*, associated so closely with colonial violence, was also replaced. From now on the army would be known as the Congolese National Army (*Armée Nationale Congolais*).

Quickly the Belgian chief of staff was replaced, and Victor Lundula appointed commander-in-chief, with Joseph Desire Mobutu, a former soldier in the *Force Publique,* becoming his deputy. The mutinies were bought under control. Mobutu had managed to persuade the majority of rebellious soldiers to return to their barracks. Though there was little violence, the mutiny terrified the European population. There was a mass exodus of state officials and white employees. But the rebellion in the army was also a key event for Lumumba. Instead of siding with Janssens and allowing the rebellion to be suppressed, Lumumba responded quite differently. He saw the mutiny as a social movement, and the refusal of soldiers to obey the orders of their white officers as a strike. This was a critical moment and Lumumba gave space for the movement to develop. Against those like Mobutu who argued that officers must be appointed from above, Lumumba defended the right of soldiers to elect their own officers.

For the Belgians the rebellion was a frightening confirmation of their fears about Lumumba. If they had begrudgingly conceded the argument for independence, maintaining control over the *Force Publique* was the one way of ensuring real power in the new state. Following the 5 July mutiny Lumumba was compelled to ask Europeans living in Matadi to leave. The women and children were removed by boat, many men stayed. These men, who had armed themselves in the run-up to independence, now opened fire on the Congolese. At least 19 dockers, workers and the unemployed were killed in the ensuing violence, and many more wounded.[143] Fearing further attacks, Congolese soldiers confiscated weapons

The leader of the breakaway province of Katanga, Moise Tshombe, reviews his new Presidential guard in Elisabethville in February 1961. The uniforms were copied directly from the French Republican Guard

from Europeans that they claimed were being held illegally. On 9 July Belgian paratroopers from the base in Kamina were dropped into Kabalo to protect Europeans who were attempting to flee. Lumumba condemned the intervention, which he saw as an effort to sabotage his government. *We have just learned that the Belgian Government has sent troops to the Congo and that they have intervened … We appeal to all Congolese to defend our Republic against all those who menace it.*[144] As he spoke more Belgian troops were landing in other cities and towns in the Congo. But these events were minor compared to what happened next.

Moise Tshombe launched an armed uprising against the new state for the independence of Katanga on 11 July, with Belgian, French and British backing. The diamond-rich South Kasai also resolved to secede; this decision was taken by Lumumba's rival

Joseph Kalonji. Lumumba was furious, he clearly saw a plot to destabilise the Congo through the dismemberment of its richest provinces. Following events confirmed Lumumba's suspicions about the role of the former colonial power. On 12 July Lumumba attempted to land at the airport in Elisabethville. Belgian officers controlling the town and airport turned off the lights making it impossible to land the plane.

Independence in Katanga was proclaimed on 11 July 1960. The new leader of Katanga, Tshombe, refused permission to both Lumumba and Kasa Vubu to travel to Elisabethville. But Tshombe's declaration of independence lacked widespread support even in Katanga. Supporters of the Prime Minister in the breakaway province organised themselves into militias to fight the secession. Jason Sendwe's BALUBAKA-BAT joined the fray against Tshombe. An agreement in 1961 for reintegrating Katanga into the country failed. Reluctant to intervene when Lumumba asked them, eventually UN troops routed Tshombe's forces and ended the secession in January 1963. The mineral-rich province had served its purpose.

Before independence, the Congo and Belgium had signed a Treaty of Friendship, Assistance and Technical Aid. Among its clauses was the agreement that no Belgian troops could intervene in the Congo, unless explicitly asked for by the new state. Ignoring this treaty, the Belgians switched allegiance to Katanga and recognised it as a legitimate state, providing an army and a commander-in-chief. The ex-colonial power worked for the break-up of the state. But behind the decision to back Katanga over the democratically-elected central government were powerful Belgian business interests. Ludo de Witte lists some of the mouths at the table: 'd'Aspremont Lynden was Lord Chamberlain at the court. He was also a commissioner of the *Société Générale de Belgique*, and administrator of the *Compagnie Maritime Belge* and the *Compagnie du Katanga*. Together with the Honorary Lord Chamberlain, Prince Amaury de Mérode represented the royal house on the college of twelve commissioners which was the ruling body of the *Société Générale* ... Deputy

Prime Minister Lilar was a former President of *Titan anversois et des Ateliers de Léopoldville*. The president of the Belgian chamber, Baron Kronacker, and Ministers Sceyven, Wigny and Albert De Vleeschauwer were administrators of a whole series of colonial enterprises.'[145]

While the Congo struggled to maintain its independence, Belgium was suffering from a political crisis at home. New tax rises of 10 billion francs, together with laws restricting trade unions were announced. By December 1960 strikes by electricity workers, port-workers and civil servants became a general strike that saw as many as 600,000 workers involved. Troops stationed in the Congo were bought home. It was only with difficulty that the strike could be broken.[146] Not only was the Belgian elite faced with the loss of its prized colonial possession, but they saw their interests threatened at home. Ludo de Witte explains how the tragedy was that 'the strikers were unable to link themselves to Lumumba, that other opponent of the Belgian government: their trade union leadership focused only on "economic" demands and made this impossible'.[147]

Lumumba wrote *Belgium intends to have Katanga, the richest province, because she cannot exist without Katanga and the Congo, as she has said.*[148] He was correct. Katanga accounted for 12 per cent of the nation's population but nearly 60 per cent of the productive resources. Officially a majority of shares in Katanga's mines were held by the state in Léopoldville. It was impossible for Lumumba, or anyone else, to permit the secession. Lumumba interpreted the secession as a Belgian-Katangan plot to split the new state up and prevent it from operating. He called on Belgian troops to withdraw, but they refused. He then asked Belgian diplomats to leave Congolese territory. He asked the UN to force the Belgians to withdraw; he hinted that it might be necessary to invite Soviet assistance. Western powers became scared. Although Lumumba was not a communist, he was seen as a potentially dangerous figure on the nationalist left. Tshombe was a completely different case. He could be trusted. Like Brussels he saw the Congo divided along ethnic lines, and he argued that it must continue to be run according to these divisions. He had also developed close ties to the Belgian business establishment whose interests were embedded in Katangan soil. The possibility of perpetuating foreign control of the highly profitable industries after independence in the Congo became a reality with the Katangan secession.

Kasa Vubu and Lumumba made a succession of appeals to the United Nations soon after the secession. Appealing initially for technical aid, they subsequently asked for direct help in ridding Congo of Belgian troops. By any reckoning the UN responded with remarkable speed, reflecting the Congo's importance in the world. UN Secretary General Dag Hammarskjöld asked the Security Council to decide on responding to the appeals for assistance against Belgian intervention. The Council agreed on military aid to the Congolese government, with the condition that force would only be used in self-defence. On 14 July the Security Council voted to send forces to the Congo. UN troops landed in Léopoldville. But over the crucial question of forcing the Belgians to withdraw the Security Council remained divided. The Russians pressed for a deadline for withdrawal, with the Americans voting against. Britain, France and China abstained. Hammarskjöld requested forces from African states and later extended the appeal to European and Asian members.

Even the conservative *Daily Telegraph*, not a natural ally of Lumumba, questioned the motives behind the secession: 'Mr. Tshombe, the self-styled President, is today far more under the domination of Belgian officials than he ever was as an obscure provincial politician before independence … Mr. Tshombe's principal speeches are being written for him by a Belgian, Mr. Thyssen, a local businessman and politician. Count Harold D'Aspremont Lynden, Chief of Cabinet to the Belgian Prime Minister, who ostensibly heads a technical aid mission, provides a link to Brussels. Colonel Champion is all but Military Commander of Katanga.'[149]

The UN in the Congo

On 14 July 1960 UN forces started to arrive in Léopoldville. Within four days there were 4,000 UN troops in the country. Though there were now plenty of troops on Congolese soil there was still no agreement whether the official mandate for 'the restoration of order' meant that Katangan secession must be suppressed. The UN mission divided. General H T Alexander, the commander of Ghana's contingent in the Congo and the British Chief of Ghana's Defence Staff, initially started to disarm members of the *Force Publique*. Lumumba stepped in, preventing further demobilisation, as for him the new Congolese National Army might need to be used against the Katangan secession.

On 20 July the Security Council met again. Dag Hammarskjöld issued the following warning: 'The United Nations has embarked on its biggest single effort under United Nations colours, organised and directed by the United Nations itself ... our attitude will be of decisive significance, I believe not only for the future of this Organisation, but also for the future of Africa. And Africa may well in present circumstances mean the world.'[150] The General Secretary was right, the Congo crisis was the first major mission that the UN had embarked on, and the eyes of the world were on the Congo. The mission determined the future role of the organisation which became at best an irritant to great powers and at worse an instrument under their control.

The Council issued a clear statement calling for an immediate Belgian withdrawal. But the problem had not been resolved. The Belgians willingly left Léopoldville by 23 July, but their forces remained very much in place in Katanga. Ghana and Guinea grew impatient. They threatened to place their troops under the authority of the central government, so they could force Katanga

Lumumba and the United Nations Secretary-General Dag Hammarskjöld met in New York on 25 July 1960. Hammarskjöld would perish in an air crash in neighbouring Northern Rhodesia (Zambia) in 1961 while on a mission to bring peace to the Congo

to obey the Lumumba-Kasa Vubu government in Léopoldville. As a consequence the UN had to decide whether to intervene in Katanga, or if a new resolution was required. In an attempt to sidestep these difficulties, Hammarskjöld visited Brussels to see if he could secure the entry of UN troops to Katanga without causing a stir. By 2 August he stated that a UN contingent would arrive in the breakaway province in three days time.

The rebel government of Katanga promised to resist. Hammarskjöld was worried about the possible use of force and believed that he needed new authority; he rushed back to New York. Katangan defiance had scared the UN away. Lumumba too was growing impatient: the body he had hoped would restore the legitimate authority of his government was vacillating wildly, and he resolved to look for African help. Yet another meeting took place at the Security Council and repeated the demand for Belgian forces to leave. Strangely the Council agreed to send troops to Katanga but ordered that they must not be used to influence internal events. This was peculiar, both recognising the authority of the Lumumba government over Katanga, but then refusing to back the possibility of force to assert this sovereignty. Back in the Congo Hammarskjöld was determined to get troops into Katanga without disturbing the balance of forces. He managed to enter the province with a nominal UN force, but refused to take a representative of Lumumba's government with him. Lumumba began to see the UN not as an ally in the crisis but as obstacle to its resolution.

External support

Lumumba now had two options. He could challenge the secession with help from outside the Congo, from African states, or look to his supporters within. From the outside he had Ghana, and the expanding ranks of the non-aligned countries increasingly describing themselves as part of the Third World. Though full of good intentions, these states delivered little. Lumumba also hoped help would come from America.

Lumumba left the Congo to solicit support from America on 22 July; but he came away with the conclusion that there was nothing to be gained from the West. President Dwight Eisenhower refused to see him, regarding him already as man lost to the Soviets. Those who spoke to him explained that they expected business to continue as usual. For years America had been buying their uranium from Belgium, and why should anything change? Lumumba responded that Belgium did not produce any uranium. America, Britain and France were hostile to him. Faced with the hardening of the secession, the failure of the UN and Western hostility, Lumumba considered turning to the Soviet Union, which had offered technical aid and military assistance. Lumumba

Patrice Lumumba photographed at London Airport on his return journey from the United Nations in August 1960

understood the risks; to pull the Soviet Union on side threatened his domestic support. Cornered, Lumumba had few choices.

But he was not isolated; he had the overwhelming support

of young nationalists and all those who had been inspired by the struggle for independence. He also had Jason Sendwe's regional support. Lumumba had enormous moral authority; he was respected more than any other politician. But each day politicians stirred up the Congo's ethnic politics, making Lumumba's hope for a unitary state harder to hold. Lumumba decided to mobilise his supporters. Ludo de Witte captures the spirit of Lumumba's strategy to make Congolese independence and freedom live. He turned towards those he was beginning to see as his most trusted allies: 'Once it became clear that the UN had taken sides with Belgium, America and Moise Tshombe to protect the secession of Katanga, which provoked the demise of the Congolese government ... Lumumba, tried to mobilise his forces. He held mass rallies of tens of thousands of people, in which he tried to explain to them that they had to organise themselves, against that neo-colonial control of Katanga ... in his public speeches, he always invited a mixed couple onto the stage, and would say: "You see these people we consider them friends, we don't want to send them away. We want the Belgians to stay, at least the Belgians who are not racist." So during the meetings, through these examples, he tried to educate people not to be anti-white, but to see things from a political perspective.'

Lumumba opened the space for the Congolese population, and at the same time stuck to a fundamental commitment to real political autonomy. Ludo de Witte claims that Lumumba's determination put in motion a revolutionary process but that there was no time in the storm of the crisis to organise a mass movement.

Possibilities were closing off fast. Though the army was now controlled by Lumumba's trusted comrade, Joseph Mobutu, events would soon break the friendship. Over the course of the two months of independence Mobutu would win the friendship of the Americans. Before long he started to receive payment from the CIA and was in contact with Western military attaches. Lumumba's natural supporters were among those urban workers loyal to his idealism but they too were weak. By the late 1940s, only 536,000 people from a population of 14 million were classed as workers. Trade union organisation was also far from solid.[151] Lumumba made no attempts to mobilise the forces of organised labour, relying instead on the power of the spoken word. This was not enough.

But all was not lost. In the middle of August the new Congolese National Army was deployed in Kivu Province and in Northern Kasai. They were ordered to crush Kalonji's secession and then move on to Katanga. The detachment in Kivu were meant to make their way directly to Katanga and link up with sympathetic groups, including Sendwe's Balubakat, and attack troops loyal to Tshombe. Initially the action was successful. A reporter from an Elisabethville paper wrote: 'In our opinion, Katanga was in its greatest danger when, towards mid-August, it was threatened in the north by two thousand Lumumbist soldiers … and by the advance of the National Army in Kasai.'[152]

But the National Army was dragged into ethnic fighting in Kasai between the Baluba and the Bena Lulua. What was originally an offensive to end the secession of Kasai and Katanga saw a series of massacres in which the Congolese National Army was involved. Abandoned by his friends and comrades Lumumba was almost completely alone. He reacted in the only honest way he could by opposing Belgium's aggression and in wanting to crush the secession of Katanga and Kasai. These decisions turned Lumumba into an unlikely revolutionary. In his 1956 book he had rejected independence as premature, and now he was almost a lone figure defending the Congo from imperialist aggression. The struggle against the disintegration of the Congo in 1960 became his real university. If Lumumba's life can be characterised by a series of sharp breaks – each pointing to a more daunting challenge ahead – then the months after June 1960 was the greatest he had faced.

Tshombe and Kalonji's fiefdom

As the UN sought to establish order in the capital, the Belgians did the same in Katanga. Tshombe received everything he needed and requested: assistance in running the mines, with royalties paid directly to him and not the central government, and technical services to help run the province. Business continued undisturbed. The payments Tshombe received were a direct breach of the agreements that were made at the Round Table Conference and accepted by, among others, Tshombe himself. These resources gave Tshombe the money to pay for a foreign army to defend Katanga, and the confidence to even threaten the UN with force.

What were the forces organising themselves in Katanga? It was common knowledge that Katanga and Tshombe's party received the backing of the Belgians. It was also an open secret that the neighbouring Central African Federation of the Rhodesias and Nyasaland backed the regime and even encouraged Tshombe to join them. But the situation inside Katanga was complex, there were serious rivals. Principally Jason Sendwe's Balubakat was strong in the region. He defended independence and the ideal of a unitary state, though Tshombe was a deft manipulator of ethnic loyalties, and played these to his advantage.

Divisions began to grow between Lumumba and Kasa Vubu. It had always been a difficult partnership, and Kasa Vubu now used Lumumba's alleged communism to engineer a break. The attack on Katanga by government forces was postponed. Belgian troops took the opportunity to help support the second breakaway state in South Kasai. The autonomous Mining State of South Kasai was declared on 8 August 1960 with its capital at Bakwanga (today's Mbuji-Mayi). Albert Kalonji was proclaimed president of new state and became the head of the government, appointing himself emperor the following year. This state also received the support of the Belgians and mining companies in the area. The Congo was splintering fast.

External forces

Another meeting of the Security Council took place on 21 August 1960 which saw a resolution offering further strong support for Dag Hammarskjöld. This resolution was opposed by the Soviet Union who began to question the objectivity of the Secretary-General, and the lack of any serious attempt to resist secession. During August, the situation continued to deteriorate, with commentators expecting a major clash between Katangan and Congolese forces.

Lumumba's patience snapped. He turned to the Soviet Union, requesting planes, trucks and weapons to crush the movements in Kasai and Katanga. There was no question of Khrushchev disagreeing. Within days of the request arriving at the Kremlin, everything that was asked for began to arrive. Larry Devlin, the CIA Station Chief in the Congo, recalled the arrival of the Soviet support: 'I had a little Congolese sitting at the airport counting any white man who came off a Soviet aircraft in batches of five. Roughly 1,000 came in during a period of six weeks. They were there as *conseillers techniques* [technical advisors] and they were posted to all the ministries. To my mind it was clearly an effort to take over. It made good sense when you stopped to think about it. All nine countries surrounding the Congo had their problems. If the Soviets could have gotten control of the Congo they could have used it as a base, bringing in Africans, training them in sabotage and military skills and sending them home to do their duty.'[153] Kasa Vubu broke from Lumumba; Mobutu also rejected the turn to the Soviet Union.

The army chief of staff rejected the authority of Soviet 'advisers' who began to lecture the army. The United States was horrified; this confirmed all their fears about Lumumba. By mid-August 1960, the Americans began to hatch a plan to replace the prime minister with a coup. In September President Khrushchev made a personal appearance at the UN General Assembly and attacked the Secretary-General. The session saw the admission of 17 new African states; they would play a role in the Congo crisis that was dividing the world body.

The cause of Katanga was defended by lobby groups in Britain, American and France. Katanga they argued was a sea of civilisation in an otherwise barbarous Congo. These arguments won many supporters in the Western business and political world. This lobbying was far less successful among African states, but still they could not decide on united action. One group of African states revolted against the UN, supporting Lumumba's plan to invade Katanga. But another remained solidly committed to the concept of UN action and sought to persuade the world-organisation to abandon negotiation in favour of direct action to end the secession.

The fall of Lumumba

Though Lumumba and Kasa Vubu had worked together presenting a united voice of condemnation against the secession of Katanga and Kasai, by September 1960 they broke. On 5 September Kasa Vubu took the first step and attempted to remove Lumumba, and appoint a new government. Lumumba rushed to parliament for support; it backed the Prime Minister, maintaining that the President had acted illegally. The political impasse was the opportunity that Mobutu and his Western backers were looking for. On 14 September, Mobutu took control in a bloodless coup, effectively removing Kasa Vubu and Lumumba. This 'peaceful revolution' as Mobutu described it, was targeted at civilian politicians who would now be given a cooling-off period. He explained that a group of the Congo's first university graduates would replace the elected government; they would form his 'College of Commissioners.' The coup leader gave Soviet personnel 48 hours to leave.

Life in Léopoldville began to reflect the collapse of political hope. According to Lumumba: *The capital of the republic is a scene of disorder, where a handful of hired military men are ceaselessly violating*

As civic order rapidly broke down in Léopoldville and many parts of the country in July 1960, Belgian settlers fled across the River Congo by ferry for the safety of Brazzaville in the former French Congo

law and order. The citizens of Léopoldville now live under a reign of terror. Arbitrary arrests, followed by deportation, are a daily and nightly occurrence ... The majority parties in Parliament are forbidden to publish newspapers. All loyal army personnel and government officials, who wanted to have no truck with the unlawful activities and the policy of national demolition pursued by the head of state and his handful of supporters at Léopoldville, have been dismissed from their posts, maltreated and turned out into the streets. Hundreds of loyal soldiers who oppose Mobutu are sent back daily to the villages: others are now in the Bina concentration camp.[154]

Andrew Cordier was Dag Hammarskjöld's new UN representative in Léopoldville. On 5 September he closed the airport and the following day he shut off the radio, which Lumumba had been using to reach his supporters. Cordier directly supervised shutting down the radio; Sallie Pisani has described what happened. 'Cordier asked the station manager how he could cut short all of these incendiary messages. The station manager quipped … "Well, you could always just steal the crystal from the transmitter" … Cordier left the station with the crystal.'[155] This immediately handed Kasa Vubu and then Mobutu an advantage. Unable to access the radio Lumumba could not appeal to his supporters and inform them about what had happened. The UN again had acted against the interests of the Congo; the action was bitterly resented across the world. It was now clear to many observers that the UN was working for the Belgians and the secessionists. This outcome suited the US perfectly. The Congo had not fallen to the Soviets. The country was for the time being in safe hands. Short of the elimination of Lumumba, Washington could not have asked for more.

As the Congo fragmented before his eyes, Lumumba's family was faced with its own tragedy. Early in November Pauline gave birth prematurely to their fourth child, a girl called Marie-Christine. As it was impossible to get proper care for the child, who was dangerously ill, the Red Cross had arranged for the mother and daughter to be sent for treatment in Geneva. They arrived too late and the child died in Switzerland. Lumumba requested permission from the UN to take her body to Stanleyville for a funeral and then burial in his home region. Permission was refused.

Patrice Lumumba was trapped. Unable to communicate with his supporters, he was confided to his Léopoldville residence. He must have known that his life was at risk. Even stripped of his political power he was still considered a threat. On 6 October, the Count d'Aspremont Lynden, responsible for African Affairs in Brussels, cabled Elisabethville, making it clear that Belgian policy now required the physical elimination of Lumumba. D'Aspremont Lynden had been the first to talk about elimination before independence. Rajeshwar Dayal took over from Andrew Cordier as the new head of the UN mission in Léopoldville. Dayal continued Cordier's work and refused to support Lumumba, turning him into a prisoner under house arrest. Finally Lumumba fled the capital on 27 November hoping to reach Stanleyville, where a government in exile was being formed.

The choice of Stanleyville was obvious. It was a city that Lumumba knew well, it was where many of his supporters and comrades were based. The city represented Lumumba with another opportunity to fight for the Congo.[156] Kemishanga was with Lumumba during his attempted escape to Stanleyville. Kemishanga was now a loyal ally of Lumumba and had been elected an MNC deputy in the national elections before independence. But what had started as a clandestine escape attempt turned into a slightly ponderous journey that included a small convoy of cars, frequent delays and impromptu speeches by Lumumba when he was recognised in the passing villages. Once the convoy had crossed into Kasai – where the MNC was well organised – they assumed there were safe. Lumumba was with his wife Pauline and youngest son Roland.

They headed to Lodi, a village on the Sankuru River. Kemishanga directed them away from the Luluabourg road, where he thought they would be found. It was late when they reached the

The day after their arrest at Port Franqui, Lumumba and Joseph Okito and Maurice Mpolo were flown from Luluabourg to Léopoldville. They are seen here being transported from the airport to be imprisoned in Thysville. 2 December 1960

river. Lumumba and Kemishanga crossed the river in a canoe and then tried to commandeer a ferry for the other members of the group still stranded on the other side. But valuable time had already been wasted and the army had been alerted to their presence. A truck carrying soldiers arrived. Kemishanga remembers Lumumba's last speech. *I know that you have been asked to kill me. But if you kill me you will not be able to sleep next to your wives. Today you obey Kasa Vubu and Mobutu but I warn you that after my death they will be your enemies. If you kill me, I will not die. If you throw me into the river, the fish will eat my flesh. The Congolese will eat the fish, and then I will be in the bellies of the people and I will never be far from my people. I will be in the belly of each Congolese. You wear stripes today, but who gave you the stripes that you wear?*

Kemishanga recalls that the soldiers looked as though they

would be swayed by his words: 'But their chief took them aside and drugged them, gave them a dose of cannabis.'[157]

Lumumba's words were not enough. Reinforcements arrived and the party was rounded up and taken to Mweka, the regional town. There was a Ghanaian contingent of the UN stationed in the town, and Lumumba immediately appealed for their intervention to prevent his removal to Léopoldville. This was denied; they had not received orders to protect him.

Lumumba was then flown to Léopoldville. Again the UN refused to intervene. Brigadier Indarjit Rikhye, the head of the UN military mission, saw him cut and bleeding, glasses broken, but 'We could not intervene', said Rikhye. They also had no authority. Lumumba was beaten in front of TV cameras. He was then sent to Thysville military barracks several hundred miles from Léopoldville. Knowing that their proxy in Katanga Moise Tshombe would carry out their orders, the Belgians insisted that Lumumba was sent to Elisabethville. Fully aware after his arrest that death was probably inevitable; Patrice Lumumba wrote a final letter to his wife. Only four months after his speech on Independence Day:

My dear companion,

I write you these words without knowing if they will reach you, when they will reach you, or if I will still be living when you read them. All during the length of my fight for the independence of my country, I have never doubted for a single instant the final triumph of the sacred cause to which my companions and myself have consecrated our lives. But what we wish for our country, its right to an honourable life, to a spotless dignity, to an independence without restrictions, Belgian colonialism and its Western allies – who have found direct and indirect support, deliberate and not deliberate, among certain high officials of the United Nations, this organization in which we placed all our confidence when we called for their assistance – have not wished it.

They have corrupted certain of our fellow countrymen, they have contributed to distorting the truth and to besmirching our independence. What else might I say? That dead, living, free, or in prison on the order of the colonialists, it is not I who counts. It is the Congo, it is our people for whom independence has been transformed into a cage where we are regarded from the outside sometimes with benevolent compassion, sometimes with joy and pleasure.

But my faith will stay unbreakable. I know and I feel to the depth of my being that sooner or later my people will get rid of all their interior and exterior enemies, that they will rise up like a single person to say no to a degrading and shameful colonialism and to reassume their dignity under a pure sun.

We are not alone. Africa, Asia, and free and liberated people from every corner of the world will always be found at the side of the Congolese. They will not abandon the fight until the day comes when there are no more colonizers and mercenaries in our country. To my children whom I leave and whom perhaps I will see no more, I wish that they be told that the future of the Congo is beautiful and that it expects from them, as it expects from each Congolese, to accomplish the sacred task of reconstruction of our independence and our sovereignty; for without dignity there is no liberty, without justice there is no dignity, and without independence there are no free men.

No brutality, mistreatment, or torture has ever forced me to ask for grace, for I prefer to die with my head high, my faith steadfast, and my confidence profound in the destiny of my country, rather than to live in submission and scorn of sacred principles. History will one day have its say, but it will not be the history that Brussels, Paris, Washington, or the United Nations will teach, but that which they will teach in the countries emancipated from colonialism and its puppets.

Africa will write its own history, and it will be, to the north and to the south of the Sahara, a history of glory and dignity.

Do not weep for me, my dear companion. I know that my country, which suffers so much, will know how to defend its independence and its liberty. Long live the Congo! Long live Africa!

Patrice[158]

The letter was meant for all Congolese. François Lumumba explains 'When he is addressing Pauline he is addressing the Congo. When he is talking to his children, he is talking to all the children of the Congo. He is telling all the children of the Congo to have confidence in the future of the country.'[159]

Joseph Okito had been a provincial advisor sitting on the regional council in Kasai between 1957–9. Though appointed by the colonial authorities he was uncompromising in his defence of the rights of the Congolese. He joined the Lumumba faction of the MNC and was elected senator on the MNC list and finally appointed vice-president of the Senate. After independence Okito accompanied Lumumba on his visit to the USA and Canada. He attempted to reach the safety of Stanleyville in November but was arrested. Described by one commentator as 'the gentle, brilliant man who had so often pleaded with his senators when they rambled off the subject'.

Finally death came. On 17 January Lumumba was flown to Elisabethville with two fellow prisoners Maurice Mpolo and Joseph Okito. Already beaten and tortured he was dragged by Katangan forces commanded by a Belgian, to *Villa Brouwe*. Here he was tortured again, as Tshombe decided how to kill him. Later in the evening they were thrown into a military vehicle and driven to a nearby wood. A Belgian officer assembled and commanded three firing squads, while another Belgian organised the execution site. Patrice Lumumba and his two comrades, Mpolo and Okito, were shot one after the other. Tshombe was present. Then Gerard Soete, a Belgian police officer, unearthed the bodies from their shallow grave, chopped each body into pieces and then dissolved them

Patrice Lumumba photographed shortly before his execution

with canisters of acid. When there was no more acid remaining the body parts were burnt. The bloody deed was done and independence had finally been broken. The Belgian government's investigation into the assassination of Lumumba in 2001 reported that 'the Belgian government deemed a speedy independence necessary in order to protect Belgian interests'.[160]

The murders were officially announced on 13 February 1961, seven and half months after independence. Lumumba was only 36 years old. The hope for a democratic and independent Congo was, for the time being, extinguished, and foreign interests could rule again. The physical obliteration of the bodies was perhaps a wish that Lumumba and his comrades would be completely forgotten and to eradicate any trace that they had ever existed. Not only were these violent murders but also an effort to rewrite history, to dissolve any memory of the hopes of a real independence. The day after the announcement of Lumumba's murder the Indonesian poet Sabarsantoso Anantaguna wrote:

Maurice Mpolo was born in 1928 in the province of Léopoldville, Mpolo worked in the colonial capital as a clerk in various private firms. In 1951 he joined the Territorial Police, but accused of arrogance and insubordination he was removed less than two years later. In the independent elections in May 1960 he was elected a deputy for the MNC. Mpolo was a fervent nationalist, who advocated radical economic reforms in an independent Congo.

The news came early in the
morning.
Lumumba is dead
Lumumba is dead
Anger split the whole world
asunder.
A worker shouts:
who can murder my age –
the rails of the trains
the length of the light of the
sun
we are all Lumumba
Lumumba.
Freedom that's Lumumba
Lumumba
The news came early in the morning
Lumumba is dead
Lumumba is dead
the earth shook
the revolution marches on.
Long live Lumumba.[161]

US Strategy and British Involvement

Who was responsible for Lumumba's downfall? Although the act of Lumumba's murder was carried out by Belgian and Katangan forces, an unholy alliance of Western interests lay behind his demise. We can name some of the guilty parties: Belgium, the United Kingdom and the United States. British Prime Minister

Harold Macmillan had joined in the fray, calling Lumumba a 'communist stooge'. Western powers had used the threat of Soviet intervention to justify their action against Lumumba; they sought to prevent the mineral-rich Congo falling into the hands of the communists. Was this a real threat? There is no question that the period was marked by vicious Cold War rivalry that was played out to devastating effect on the continent. But Lumumba was no communist, rather a nationalist who sought meaningful independence in a world that refused it. His insistence on political autonomy was almost regarded as juvenile and he was denounced as unstable and mad. The Tanzanian radical Abdulrahman Mohamed Babu was clear about the extent of Soviet involvement at the time of independence, 'when the Congo stormed into independence in 1960, the only contact the Soviet Union had with that country was through a Czechoslovakian trade representative who was so ill-informed about what was going on in the country that he gave the Kremlin a completely wrong picture of the situation.'[162] In fact, what Devlin has written about Soviet intervention, advisors and aircraft is nonsense: according to archival research all internal messages, telexes and reports contradict this. Devlin's assertion that there was a KGB agent is also utterly unfounded; there was no such Soviet spy inside Lumumba's government.

All over Africa nations claimed their independence at an astonishing speed. Following defeat at Suez Britain rapidly decolonised. France resisted for a little longer, but in 1958 granted a whole group of African countries a form of independence and only remained in Algeria for a bloody fight. New powers were preparing to play a role in a decolonised Africa. The United States retained something of the allure of freedom, because of the country's undeniable opposition to the French and British project of re-capturing the Suez Canal after its nationalization by President Nasser of Egypt in 1956. At the expense of the British, French and Belgians American influence was growing on the continent.

But Washington rejected Lumumba principally for his 'extreme nationalism'. They refused to cooperate with him when he arrived in the US and helped force him to turn to the Soviet Union. There is no evidence that the Congo was, as Devlin described, a 'Cuba in the making'.[163] Devlin actively assisted Mobutu, promoting him as a prodigal son. The intention was to prevent Soviet intrusion, and ensure Lumumba's downfall. Devlin worked with Mobutu during his September coup and regarded Lumumba as a dangerous obstacle: 'We came to the conclusion that he was rather unbalanced. From one moment to the other he could change. We saw him as someone who thought he could use the Soviets and the Soviets in turn were trying to use him, and we felt that they were much more experienced and qualified at this act than Lumumba. It was his first coup on 14 September 1960. I agreed that we would help him … the objective was to prevent the Soviets from gaining undue influence in the country. They had one minister who was definitely a KGB agent. I hoped that by using the "service" intelligence methods we could avoid a hot war, particularly an atomic hot war.'[164]

What, of course, is extraordinary is that if Lumumba could be dismissed as 'rather unbalanced' for even entertaining the possibility of Soviet assistance then why was Tshombe, who was openly dependant on Belgian military forces, left to his own devices? But as a loyal member of NATO Belgium was a friendly foreign power, the Russians were not.

There was never any possibility that the Congo would be left to work out its own independence. Cursed by mineral wealth the country could not be left alone. Uranium from the Congo was regularly bought through Belgium by the Americans and it had already been used to make the atomic bombs dropped on Japan at the end of the Second World War. But now cobalt was discovered and memoranda sent back to the US stating that it was an essential metal needed for the space race between the Americans and the Soviets. American interests had for many decades been central to the political economy of the Congo. In the early 1950s, a company owned by the Rockefeller family had taken control of a one-fifth share in *Union Minière*, the business that ran the uranium mines.[165]

So American intervention was crucial. President Eisenhower sanctioned the assassination of Lumumba. 'The President would have vastly preferred to have him taken care of some other way than by assassination, but he regarded Lumumba as I did and as a lot of other people did as a mad dog … and he wanted the problem dealt with.'[166] Devlin was given instructions to assassinate Lumumba, they came from the president. 'I was told that instructions came from President Eisenhower. The president had implied that something must be done and his words were taken as an indication that he wanted an assassination.' Devlin received a consignment of poison to carry out these orders: 'I received a cable to the effect that an officer would be coming to see me. I was told that the man would identify himself as "Joe from Paris". As I left the embassy for the café across the street … seated … was a … man I knew quite well. He got up and started to move towards my car … I took him to a safe house. And once we got moving he said: "I'm Joe from Paris". When we got there he told me that he had brought instructions that I must assassinate Lumumba. He gave me a packet of poisons, various sorts … one … came in toothpaste.'[167]

Further evidence of Britain's desire to see Lumumba murdered has recently come to light. Daphne Park, a former British intelligence officer, claimed before she died in 2010 that Britain played a central role in Lumumba's assassination. She was an MI6 officer in the Belgian Congo from 1959. Before she died Park's told a fellow member of the House of Lords that she had helped to co-ordinate Britain's role in Lumumba's murder in 1961. In a conversation with David Lea – Baron Lea of Crondall – in 2009, she made the revelation: 'I was having a cup of tea with Daphne Park – we were colleagues from opposite sides of the Lords – a few months before she died in March 2010. She had been consul and first secretary in Leopoldville, now Kinshasa, from 1959 to 1961, which in practice (this was subsequently acknowledged) meant head of MI6 there. I mentioned the uproar surrounding Lumumba's abduction and murder, and recalled the theory that MI6 might have had something to do with it. 'We did,' she replied, 'I organised it.'[168]

Given the media attention that this 'revelation' caused in 2013, it is important for us to reflect for a moment on Park's assertion. Park's boast that 'we' did it is a case of wishful thinking. Britain was involved in hatching a plot to eliminate Lumumba, but they did not 'organise it' or 'do it.' Foreign Office minutes from September 1960 indicate that while there was serious consideration of 'eliminating' Lumumba, these were still largely speculative. On 28 September HFT Smith, a member of the African Department of the Foreign Office, made his recommendations clear, 'I see only two possible solutions to the problem. The first is the simple one of ensuring Lumumba's removal from the scene by killing him .... The other possible approach is for a constitution to be worked out ... Of these two possibilities, my preference ... would be for Lumumba to be removed from the scene altogether.' His senior colleagues agreed, concurring that a constitutional solution would not be an effective 'remedy.'[169] For a number of global powers there was an astonishing rush to kill the Congo's first leader, though not surprisingly it was the ex-colonial power that had the logistical knowledge to carry it out. As we have seen the Belgian's got there first.

In the end the Belgians were better organised. But the implication implicit in Devlin's confession and the UK Foreign Office minutes at the time, is that the Americans and/or the British would have carried out the assassination, perhaps using a Congolese proxy, if the Belgians had not beaten them to it.

Pan-Africanism and the UN

The UN also played an important part in Lumumba's fall. The

organisation was not immune from the imperial objectives of some of its powerful member states, nor was it simply an empty vessel to be filled by the unequal weight of its affiliates. The international organisation was an important actor in the events that were unfolding in the Congo. While it is clear that soon after independence, the US, France, Britain and Belgium discussed the definitive elimination of Lumumba, no longer simply his political elimination, similar views and plans were held by senior members of the UN hierarchy. Lumumba himself was clear about the role of the organisation: *Belgian colonialism and its Western allies have found direct and indirect support ... among certain high officials of the United Nations.*[170] The UN's hands were bloodied.

There were other false friends. Lumumba had placed enormous faith in pan-Africanism. In the first week of August 1960 he visited a number of African states, already independent, and who seemed to be offering him practical assistance. He returned to Leopoldville convinced that the promises made by various heads of state would be upheld, and that pan-Africanism would cease to be a slogan and become instead a plan of action for the defence of the Congo. Ghana and Guinea promised to place their troops under his control if the UN failed to expel the foreign forces and end the secession. A pan-African conference was planned for the capital on 25 August. Thirteen independent African states sent their representatives, but mostly only ambassadors attended. Delegate after delegate praised the behaviour of the UN and refused any practical help to the central government. For Lumumba the conference was another illusion destroyed.

Kwame Nkrumah, a confidant of Lumumba's since 1958, sent a stream of fatherly communiqués to Lumumba preaching conciliation and compromise long after these had ceased to be possible. On 12 September he wrote: 'You cannot afford, my Brother, to be harsh and uncompromising. Do not force Kasa Vubu out now [Kasa Vubu had already 'removed' Lumumba in a coup on

African Americans demonstrate outside the United Nations building in New York at the news of his assassination in February 1961

5 September]. It will bring too much trouble in Léopoldville … Be as "cool as a cucumber" … Patrice … if you fail, you have only yourself to blame … Your policy "to do away with your enemies now" will fail; you must adopt "TACTICAL ACTION."'[171]

It must have been particularly galling for Lumumba to receive 'cucumber' advice from his respect comrade and fellow pan-Africanist. Lumumba wrote angrily to Nkrumah on 11 September explaining to his friend the role that Ghanaian troops were playing in the unfolding crisis: *At 4.30 p.m today, 11 September, accompanied by my soldiers, I personally went to take over the radio station. The Ghana troops, however, opposed my decision with hostility and went to the extent of seizing arms from my soldiers … Instead of helping us in our difficulties; your soldiers are openly siding with the enemy to fight us.*[172] But Nkrumah's role in the crisis illustrated a fundamental weakness in the politics of pan-Africanism, which infected Lumumba's own political decisions. Nkrumah repeatedly cautioned against mobilising the population, and pressed instead for resolutions through the UN.

But the UN had taken a position against Lumumba. So as his friends insisted on confidence in the international body, Lumumba was languishing under house arrest from the same UN in Léopoldville. By October he abandoned all hope of a solution through the organisation. Ludo de Witte's is correct in apportioning blame: 'All this has to do with the pressure of so-called "pan-Africanism" and from people like Nkrumah, who was very conservative.'[173] Nkrumah's pan-Africanism sought to effect change through diplomatic channels, long after these channels had been exhausted. The revolutionary rhetoric that had attracted Lumumba to pan-Africanism when he had first visited Ghana in 1958 seemed increasingly vacuous. In the end Lumumba turned to his second option: mobilising his own supporters in the Congo. But by the time he had escaped from the capital valuable time had been lost.

Pauline Lumumba photographed with her youngest son Roland and her brother-in-law shortly after the assassination of her husband Patrice

Lumumba: liberation hero

Patrice Lumumba's murder was met with an explosion of protests. In Shanghai, a demonstration estimated at half a million held a rally against the murder. Demonstrators in Belgrade shouted,

'Lumumba will live for ever'. For President Tito the murder of Lumumba 'had no precedent in latter day history'. In Yugoslavia as many as 30,000 smashed their way into the Belgian embassy in Belgrade. In Warsaw demonstrators attacked the Belgian Embassy forcing the Ambassador to flee for his life. A session of the Italian Chamber of Deputies in Rome descended into chaos as demonstrators broke up the proceedings, then threatened to march on the Belgian embassy. In their thousands Syrian students join workers demonstrating in the city's streets.[174] There were also protests in London and Paris.

In the meeting rooms of the UN in New York there was a potent sense of shame and seething anger. The journalist Philip Deane wrote: 'In small private wakes for Patrice Lumumba, the Afro-Asian delegates … swallow their drinks as if there were a bitter taste in their mouths … They may not all have felt such concern for Lumumba alive and active … but … in the lobbies and corridors and bars of the United Nation's glass palace, you can hear growing almost hour by hour a menacing myth that could destroy the world organisation itself.'[175]

But in much of the Congo there was silence and disbelief. Those new leaders who were now in control of the Congo sought desperately to keep the news from breaking out. There could be no funerals, the bodies of Lumumba, Okito and Mpolo had been destroyed. Pauline Opango, Lumumba's wife, marched at the head of a procession of about 100 people in Léopoldville. Only in Luluabourg, the city that had seen the first proud congress of the MNC in 1959, was a general strike organised to protest against the killings. 'But in Stanleyville, where the armed nationalists had begun the apparently unstoppable reconquest of the country, the announcement of the death of Lumumba, Mpolo and Okito produced no immediate visible reactions. On the contrary, a deathly, supernatural calm fell over the city, as if Lumumba's death could not be true, as if Lumumba's personality had already taken on the mythical proportions it would assume in the decades to come.' A great Mass was held in the town on 16 February for Lumumba. Twenty-five thousand people attended and then returned home peacefully.[176]

The Belgian press barely concealed their howls of approval. *La Libre Belgique* who had led the propaganda campaign against Lumumba when he was alive stated on 14 February that he 'was a cruel man, unable to govern, even to govern himself ... he sowed fire and blood wherever he went. .. Politics was nothing other than an exciting game ... The game turned out badly for him.'[177]

Three of Lumumba's children were already in Egypt where they had been invited by President Nasser. François, Patrice and Juliana were told the news of their father's murder by their host family in Cairo. François explains that although the children knew the situation was serious when they left the Congo, they were convinced that they would see their father again, 'we had the conviction that our father would live'.[178] They learnt of the news at the same time as the rest of the world. Juliana remembers: 'We were already in Egypt, in Cairo and it was one month after his murder, as it was for everyone. Our Egyptian father brought us together to tell us that our father was dead. It was curious because we heard people in the street demonstrating, everyone crying our name ... we could hear "Lumumba, Lumumba". I was often ill as a young child, but a car was sent for Patrice and François so they could be shown to the demonstrators, protected by soldiers, of course, who always guarded us. They moved around the city. I remember how strange it was to hear our name chanted by the crowd.'[179] François remembers how they were 'invited onto the podium' during the demonstrations and how they became symbols for the struggle against imperialism.

Lumumba's Legacy

On 14 September 1960 Joseph Mobutu seized power in Léopoldville. He dissolved parliament and expelled the Russian and Czech embassies and advisors from the country, and later declared for Kasa Vubu, who became his willing accomplice.[180] Mobutu was the *de facto* power in the capital, and as Lumumba struggled to organise his supporters, he plotted the future of the country with his foreign backers. Although he had nominally handed over power to a group of Congolese university graduates, he remained the real power behind the scenes. Independence had splintered. There had been now four separate governments operating within months of independence. The US supported the government in Léopoldville, another in Katanga and Kasai supported by the Belgians and later in the year one run by supporters of Lumumba in Stanleyville. The break-up of the Congo was a fact. In this state of general collapse Mobutu could play a decisive role in his country's future. Among Congolese politicians involved in Lumumba's murder Mobutu was a key figure. He was seen by the CIA operative in Léopoldville as a charming and affable intermediary. He understood and did not seek to challenge the Congo's place in the international hierarchy of power. Mobutu introduced a new constitution and some kind of order. Though supported by the West, which lavished money and support on him, Mobutu could not establish proper control of regions outside the capital. Even the army that he controlled was divided. This instability meant that the alliance that had been

Lumumba in conversation with Mobutu in 1960. Mobutu seized power in a coup d'etat in 1965, and remained leader of the Congo until his overthrow in 1997

made between Mobutu and Kasa Vubu did not hold; in February 1961 a new government was appointed under the leadership of Joseph Ileo.[181]

But the Ileo coalition lasted just six months until August, when Cyrille Adoula succeeded Ileo and remained at the head of the government until 1964. Throughout this period the Lumumbists led by Antoine Gizenga tried to survive in Stanleyville, while Tshombe ran Katanga until the beginning of 1963. The Stanleyville government never found the same level of support for their breakaway in Kasai, as Tshombe had in Katanga. It developed after Lumumba and Kasa Vubu split and after Lumumba's murder. The exiled government was led by Pierre Mulele and Christophe Gbenye, who had been ministers in Lumumba's government, and

Antoine Gizenga

Gaston Soumaliot who was a militant Lumumbist. Their attempts to resist the Katangan secession and the unelected government in Léopoldville won popular support in different parts of the country. Stanleyville became the headquarters of the Popular Government of the Congo, claiming, with considerable legitimacy, to being the true government of the country. Their support divided along Cold War lines, and they were applauded by the Soviet Union and China.

But the victory over Lumumba gave enormous confidence to those who had assisted in his murder in 1961; they sought to press home their advantage. Tshombe recruited foreign mercenaries on vast salaries to deal with the insurgency in Stanleyville. A motley army of foreign fighters marched on the insurgent city, killing whenever they could. One mercenary later commented: 'Sometimes we killed in a frenzy ... We all seemed to be turned

Rioters in Elisabethville stone a UN armoured car following the news that the organisation had vetoed the use of mercenary troops in the territory

into wild, rampaging animals.'[182] Thousands of nationalists were killed in North Katanga by the secessionist army at the end of 1960 and the beginning of 1961.

The effort to rid the Congo of Lumumba's supporters continued from 1960 to 1964. After the rebellion in Kwilu in 1964 was crushed Pierre Mulele went into hiding. The government offered a massive bounty for information that would lead to his arrest, but no one spoke. There followed a savage campaign against the remaining resistance with Belgian and American intervention at the end of the year, in their wake Mobutu's troops killed tens of thousands of people in the east and northeast of the country. By the end of 1964 victory over the Lumumbists was complete. Mobutu's second coup in 1965 consecrated the new order. Tricked by a promise of amnesty in 1968, Mulele returned to Kinshasa and was arrested, refused a trial and swiftly executed. Mulele's execution mimicked the brutality shown to Lumumba seven years previously; he was cut into pieces while he was still alive, bundled into a sack and then drowned in the Congo River.

Those leaders who betrayed the Congo's independence gained only the ignominy of history. Tshombe's brief tenure at the head of secessionist Katanga was marked by corruption and discontent. After his fall from power he lived in exile for a number of years in Spain. Mobutu returned to the political scene with a second coup on 24 November 1965, declaring an end to the rule of politicians. Mobutu ordered a trial of Tshombe that condemned him *in absentia* to death for treason. In the end Tshombe was kidnapped in 1967 and delivered to Algeria where he died in prison of a heart attack two years later. Mobutu continued to rule the Congo until 1997, supported by an almost unbroken flow of money from the West. America continued to be Mobutu's most loyal ally. Under his control the Congo remained a source of enormous profits for western interests, and a place of unremitting hardship for most Congolese.

Children of violence

What happened to Lumumba's family after the assassination? In October 1960 Juliana, François and Patrice were sent to Egypt. The following year they were joined by their mother Pauline and their youngest brother Roland. The children ended up completing their schooling in Egypt. Initially Lumumba had considered Ghana as the place of exile, but as François explains he settled on Egypt, 'because it had been independent longer and he perceived it as more stable.'[183] They were the guests of President Nasser. It was an intensely political environment, their house receiving visitors from movements still fighting for independence. François remembers how they became symbols for the struggle against imperialism: 'When there was a visiting African Head of State who passed through Egypt they often asked to see the children of Lumumba. They would ask us if we needed anything.'[184]

Juliana describes the world in which they grew up. 'We stayed with a very nationalist, revolutionary family. In Egypt we lived in an environment where we were reminded constantly that we were the children of the nationalist hero Lumumba. And we always knew that behind the murder were international forces. But we benefited from a certain distance, far from the Congo and Belgium we did not grow up with hate. We knew of course that Belgium was involved in the assassination of our father but that it was the Belgian state and not the Belgian people.'[185]

All the children went to French boarding schools, which had been their father's wish. Before they left the Congo Lumumba had spoken to his eldest son François and explained that they must speak French together. He said that though they might be educated abroad, none of the children must ever forget that the Congo was their home and that they had a responsibility to return. 'As his eldest son he told me that as soon as we were finished with our studies we should return to the Congo. He said: *You have to hold onto your country*'.[186]

Guy Lumumba, Patrice's last child, filed a case in 2010 against certain men in Belgium who were involved in his father's murder. In late 2012 an appeals court in Brussels ruled that Belgian prosecutors could investigate Lumumba's assassination. Lumumba's last born made a powerful case for the prosecution, 'We are targeting the assassins … They are alive and we want them to answer for their ignoble acts ….' Commenting on his father's death, Guy Lumumba explained, 'It is a father I am looking for, a father whom I still love, and I want to know why he was killed.'[187]

All his children eventually returned to the Congo. Juliana finished her schooling in Egypt and then studied in France, François completed his university education in economics and politics in Hungary and Patrice studied architecture in Paris. All the children were marked by their father's politics. François describes their childhood in the Congo: 'It was a period where we lived only with adults and we didn't live as children'. Forced to leave the country, hidden in a military jeep and then flown secretly to a foreign country where they could not speak a word of the language. Forever separated from their father, without their mother. They were the children of violence. The murder of their father still casts its long shadow over their lives.

Class and liberation

The fact that no one moved to stop Lumumba's murder points to an awkward reality. Despite the universal popularity of Patrice Lumumba among the people of the Congo in July 1960, his regime and his ideal of a unitary and independent Congo was toppled in less than a year. Most Congolese did little to stop his killing. The people of the Congo wanted Lumumba to live but they lacked the knowledge, the techniques of popular struggle and organisation that might have saved him. Lumumba, and his general political orientation, bears some of the responsibility for this failure.

The MNC that was built in a frenzy of political excitement in the year before independence was essentially limited to the mobilisation for national liberation. It was also a party built by the *évolués* and most of the principle positions of deputies, advisors and organisers were members of the same petty bourgeoisie. This class was happy to remain parasitical to foreign interests and money. Writing in 1963 Jean-Paul Sartre noted how Lumumba appointed 'without the least suspicion the most active elements of his class … men whose common interest predisposed them to betray him.'[188]

The MNC had neither organisational roots across the Congo that could have defended Lumumba nor an ideological head that could have fought for a country free of exploitation, linked to a regional project of political transformation. Many of Lumumba's supporters were trade unionists, mine workers and the urban unemployed who had become radicalised in the fight for independence but these groups were never at the centre of the MNC's politics. On the contrary these forces – that could have paralysed the country's mining facilities – were seen as minor players who could apply pressure on Belgian interests but not become a political alternative in their own right. Sartre believed that Lumumba needed to 're-immerse himself in the masses, break with the *évolués*; give a social element to his politics of unity'. Finally the Congolese were left without an organisation which could have fought for unity 'in the struggle against exploitation'.[189]

Popular forces that were active in the movement had not been able to impose themselves over the warring interests of the Congolese *évolués*. Sartre's conclusion was harsh: 'without organisation, without a revolutionary programme, this brutal radicalisation of independence arrived at nothing.'[190] These are not abstract criticisms made with the benefit of hindsight but important debates that preoccupied Congolese politics and commentators at the time. Sartre pondered what might have happened: 'if Patrice had lived, who knows if, disappointed by his class, he had taken a stand against them.'[191]

When Lumumba attempted to defend Congolese independence in August 1960 he was left with his only weapon, described by Sartre as the 'dictatorship of the spoken word'. Potent though his words were, they were incapable of confronting the organised resistance to independence that was amassing around him. On 20 February 1961 Fanon wrote of his comrade's attempts to mobilise his supporters: 'Each time his enemies emerged in a region of the Congo to raise opinion against him, it was only necessary for Lumumba to appear, to explain and to denounce for the situation to return to normal. He forgot that he could not be everywhere at the same time and that the miracle of the explanation was less the truth of what he exposed then the truth of his person.'[192]

Lumumba could not substitute himself for a popular movement which might have envisaged a defence of independence based on the power of the Congolese urban and rural poor. The politics of national liberation – stripped of any notion of the class-struggle – limited Lumumba's ability to defend independence. Still the chances of an anti-capitalist politics – suggested by both Fanon and Sartre – emerging in the context of the decolonisation of the Congo were slight.

Lumumba sought independence for the Congo in a world dominated by the power of a few states and in the middle of the Cold War. The Congolese economy was inextricably global, linked perhaps more than any ex-colony through its enormous mineral wealth to chains of economic command in the West. Washington saw the country as a source of cheap uranium and increasingly cobalt, and for Brussels enormous riches came from control of mining in Katanga and Kasai. Neither of these countries was prepared to contemplate any real transformation of the Congo's role in the world. For France and Britain the Congo could not be allowed genuine autonomy, which might have turned the country into a model for other emerging nations.

Revolutionary hero

Ludo de Witte writes that the biography of Lumumba is the story of the transition 'from nationalist to revolutionary'. Lumumba was a revolutionary not in the terms of his nationalist programme, which was not particularly radical. But he sought to implement the process of decolonisation completely; as a consequence 'he provoked a revolutionary dynamic in society, in which he answered positively.'[193] This took place in his struggle against the secession of South Kasai and Katanga, his refusal to compromise with Mobutu, his attempts to mobilise ordinary Congolese to rise up in defence of the new state and then finally in his attempt to re-establish a Congolese government from nationalist Stanleyville. Lumumba was known all over the world, hated by some as a dangerous communist and adored by many as a figure of anti-imperialist resistance.

Lumumba's murder was not inevitable, and his defence of

independence not futile. On the contrary at the end of August there was still considerable hope: the Kasai secession had been broken, the army was invading the north of Katanga, while in central Katanga pro-Lumumbist forces were rebelling against the secession. For a time there was the possibility of a military victory. So Lumumba's behaviour was not foolhardy as critics even today maintain. While many of his comrades collapsed faced with the obstacles to Congolese independence in 1960, Lumumba radicalised.

But Lumumba made a number of serious mistakes. The first was his decision to turn to the United Nations. The second error is that he was initially over-confident in his ability to resolve the crisis through parliament. So after the first *coup d'état* by his president Joseph Kasa Vubu on 5 September, he did not prepare for a clash with pro-Belgian forces, because he was confident of his majority in parliament. But the situation was decided outside parliament. Lumumba's final error was that he waited until the end of November to attempt a serious mobilisation of his supporters in the east. This gave his enemies in Katanga vital time to organise themselves. However the odds against Lumumba were huge, his opponents swarming all around him: in 2001 the Belgian commission of inquiry into his murder identified four different operations underway to assassinate him.

Despite this commentators showered his death with stern reprimands. The most audacious of these came from Colin Legum, who wrote in 1962 about Lumumba's unstable character. Apparently 'Lumumba had an inflexible mind. This obduracy was made more difficult by his emotional mind'. During the crisis: 'It was unnerving. Incessantly he would repeat his own arguments over and over again.' But worst of all Lumumba 'saw enemies everywhere. In the end they destroyed him.'[194]

By September most Western leaders wanted Lumumba dead, which was also the explicit and public objective of his opponents

A statue commemorating Patrice Lumumba as a national hero in Kinshasa

in the Congo. By the end of September he had faced two coups, one led by the president and another by his former collaborator and friend Mobutu. The country was awash with mercenaries and Belgian troops and Lumumba was condemned by half the world's press as a 'mad dog' and communist. The UN that had been invited into the Congo in the expectation that it would end the illegal Belgian-supported secession of Katanga, placed Lumumba in 'protective custody' and worked on behalf of the West. In the Congo in 1960 identifying 'enemies everywhere' was a fairly rudimentary exercise of political observation, and certainly not a symptom of advanced paranoia. Even today the perception of Lumumba as unstable and ultimately responsible for his own demise finds it way into numerous accounts of the Congo crisis.[195]

Lumumba is still celebrated today for his consistent and determined resistance to any attempt to usurp independence. He refused to compromise with the external forces that sought to continue the plunder of the Congo after 30 June 1960. Nor did he attempt to make deals with members of the *évolués*, who sought the continuity of foreign occupation and control. In the face of obstacles Lumumba became more radical, and in the process he edged towards a criticism of the nationalism that he had spent the last years of his life championing. His son François describes his father's evolution in the last year of his life: 'He was a pragmatist but he started to move beyond the spirit of nationalism. He discovered in the course of 1960 that not all Congolese had the same interpretation of independence, our "brothers" were fighting for something completely different. So in his actions and in his speeches he became more precise and spoke of workers, justice and equality. How can you have political independence without economic independence? Was independence simply a national flag while economic power rests in the hands of foreign powers?'[196]

All attempts to destroy the example of Lumumba's uncompromising defence of the Congo's independence have failed and he remains the undimmed hero of African liberation.

Notes

1. J Van Lierde (ed), *Lumumba speaks: The speeches and writings of Patrice Lumumba 1958–1961* (Boston: Little, Brown and Company, 1972), pp. 220–1.
2. Michela Wrong, *In the footsteps of Mr Kurtz* (London: Fourth Estate, 2000), p. 33.
3. H M Stanley, *The Congo and the founding of its free state: a story of work and exploration* 2 vols (London: Sampson Low, Marston, Searle and Rivington, 1885) vol. II, p. 356.
4. A Hochschild, *King Léopold's Ghost: A Story of Greed, Terror and Heroism in Colonial Africa* (London: Pan Books, 1998), p. 63.
5. Hochschild, *King Léopold's Ghost*, p. 72.
6. Ludo de Witte, interview (Brussels), 19 June 2006.
7. D Renton, D Seddon and L Zeilig, *The Congo: Plunder and Resistance* (London: Zed Books, 2006), pp. 25–6.
8. Mark Twain, *King Léopold's Soliloquy: a defence of his Congo rule*, (Boston M. A: P. R Warren, 1905), p. 23.
9. Hochschild, *King Léopold's Ghost*, p. 233.
10. *Encyclopédie du Congo Belge: Tome I* (Brussels: Éditions Bieleveld, 1950), p. 39.
11. R Segal, *African Profiles* (London: Penguin, 1962), p. 180.
12. J Polasky, *The Democratic Socialism of Emile Vandervelde: Between Reform and Revolution* (Oxford: Berg, 1995), p. 59.

13. Nzongola-Ntalaja, *The Congo from Leopold to Kabila: A people's History* (London: Zed Books, 2002), pp. 31–2.
14. J Omasombo and B Verhaegem, 'Patrice Lumumba: Jeunesse et apprentissage politique 1925–1956', *Cahiers Africains*, 33–34 (1998), p. 55, hereafter Omasombo and Verhaegem, 'Jeunesse et apprentissage'.
15. Quoted in Omasombo and Verhaegem, 'Jeunesse et apprentissage', p. 56.
16. Quoted in Omasombo and Verhaegem, 'Jeunesse et apprentissage', pp. 61–3.
17. P Lumumba, *Congo, my country* (New York: Frederick A. Praeger, 1962), p. 82
18. Lumumba, *Congo, my country*, p. 69.
19. M Mamdani, *Understanding the Crisis in Kivu* (Dakar: CODESRIA, 2001), p. 4
20. Mamdani, *Understanding the Crisis in Kivu*, p. 4.
21. C Perrys, *Black Mineworkers in Central Africa: Industrial Strategies and the Evolution of an African Proletariat in the Copperbelt 1911–1941* (London: Heinemann, 1979), p. 58.
22. M D Markovitz, *Cross and Sword: The political role of Christian missions in the Belgian Congo 1908–1960* (Stanford CA: Hoover Institution Press, 1973), pp. 22, 26, 115.
23. J Gérard-Libois, 'The New Class and Rebellion in the Congo', *Socialist Register* (1966), pp. 267–80, 267.
24. M D Markovitz, *Cross and Sword*, p. 104.
25. M Ewans, *European Atrocity, African Catastrophe: Leopold II, the Congo Free State and its Aftermath* (London: Routledge, 2000), pp. 238–42.
26. Juliane Lumumba, interview (Kinshasa), 18 November 2006.
27. Quoted in Omasombo and Verhaegem, 'Jeunesse et apprentissage', pp. 83–5.

28. Quoted in Omasombo and Verhaegem, 'Jeunesse et apprentissage', p. 94.
29. Quoted in Omasombo and Verhaegem, 'Jeunesse et apprentissage', pp. 97–8.
30. Lumumba, *Congo, my country*, pp. 108–9.
31. Lumumba, *Congo, my country*, p. 87
32. L Kapita Mulopo, *P. Lumumba: Justice pour le héros* (Paris: l'Harrmattan, 1992), p. 31.
33. C D Young, *Politics in the Congo: Decolonization and Independence* (Princeton: Princeton University Press, 1963), pp. 11, 93–4.
34. Tony Busselen, interview (Kinshasa), 18 November 2006.
35. Perrys, *Black Mineworkers*, pp. 225–7; J Higginson, *A Working Class in the Making: Belgian Colonial Labor Policy, Private Enterprise, and the African Mineworker 1907–1951* (Wisconsin: University of Wisconsin Press, 1989), p. 193.
36. Juliane Lumumba, interview (Kinshasa), 18 November 2006.
37. Omasombo and Verhaegem, 'Jeunesse et apprentissage', p. 111–2.
38. Quoted in Omasombo and Verhaegem, 'Jeunesse et apprentissage', p. 114.
39. Quoted in Omasombo and Verhaegem, 'Jeunesse et apprentissage', pp. 123–4.
40. Quoted in Mulopo, *P. Lumumba: Justice pour le héros*, p. 40.
41. Quoted in Omasombo and Verhaegem, 'Jeunesse et apprentissage', p. 127.
42. Quoted in Omasombo and Verhaegem, 'Jeunesse et apprentissage', p. 127.
43. Juliana Lumumba, interview (Kinshasa), 18 November 2006.
44. Quoted in Omasombo and Verhaegem, 'Jeunesse et apprentissage', pp. 136–7.

45. Quoted in Omasombo and Verhaegem, 'Jeunesse et apprentissage', p. 137.
46. Quoted in Omasombo and Verhaegem, 'Jeunesse et apprentissage', p. 137.
47. Quoted in Omasombo and Verhaegem, 'Jeunesse et apprentissage', pp. 137–8.
48. Quoted in Omasombo and Verhaegem, 'Jeunesse et apprentissage', p. 139.
49. Juliane Lumumba, interview (Kinshasa), 18 November 2006.
50. Lumumba, *Congo, my country*, pp. 120–1.
51. Lumumba, *Congo, my country*, p. 115.
52. Juliana Lumumba, interview (Kinshasa), 18 November 2006.
53. François Lumumba, interview (Kinshasa), 20 November 2006.
54. Lumumba, *Congo, my country*, p. 114.
55. Gérard-Libois, 'The New Class and Rebellion in the Congo', p. 270.
56. D N Gibbs, *The Political Economy of Third World Intervention: Mines, Money and US policy in the Congo Crisis* (Chicago: university of Chicago Press, 1991), p. 57.
57. Tony Busselen, interview (Kinshasa), 18 November 2006.
58. T Cliff, 'Deflected Permanent Revolution' in *International Socialism* 1(1963) p. 20.
59. Panaf Great Lives, *Patrice Lumumba* (London: Panaf, 1973), p. 196.
60. Lumumba, *Congo, my country*, p. 91.
61. Quoted in Omasombo and Verhaegem 'Jeunesse et apprentissage', p. 183.
62. Quoted in Omasombo and Verhaegem, 'Jeunesse et apprentissage', p. 155.

63. Quoted in J M Makombo, 'Patrice Lumumba – Correspondant de presse: 1948–1956', *Cahiers Africains*, 3 (1993), pp. 24–5, hereafter Makombo, 'Correspondant de presse'.
64. Quoted in Makombo, 'Correspondant de presse', p.26.
65. Quoted in Omasombo and Verhaegem, 'Jeunesse et apprentissage', p. 193.
66. P de Vos, *Vie et mort de Lumumba* (Paris: Calmann-Levy, 1961), p. 30.
67. Lumumba, *Congo, my country*, p. 51.
68. Quoted in Omasombo and Verhaegem, 'Jeunesse et apprentissage', p. 202.
69. De Vos, *Vie et mort de Lumumba*, p. 46.
70. Lumumba, *Congo, my country*, p. 172.
71. Lumumba, *Congo, my country*, p.19.
72. Quoted in J Omasombo and B Verhaegem, 'Acteur politique: de la prison aux portes du pouvoir. Juillet 1956 – février 1960' *Cahiers Africains*, 68–69–70 (2005), p. 27, hereafter Omasombo and Verhaegem, 'Acteur politique'.
73. Quoted in Omasombo and Verhaegem, 'Acteur politique', pp.29–30.
74. Quoted in Omasombo and Verhaegem, 'Acteur politique', p. 41.
75. Quoted in Omasombo and Verhaegem, 'Acteur politique', p. 69.
76. Lumumba, *Congo, my country*, p. 77.
77. Lumumba, *Congo, my Congo*, pp. 1–2.
78. R Mckown, *Lumumba: a biography* (New York: Doubleday, 1969), p. 52.
79. Quoted in Omasombo and Verhaegem, 'Acteur politique', pp. 66–7.
80. Lumumba, *Congo, my country*, p. 187.
81. Lumumba, *Congo, my country*, p. 81

82. Lumumba, *Congo, my country*, pp. 94, 178.
83. Lumumba, *Congo, my country*, p. 135.
84. Lumumba, *Congo, my country*, p. 155, 169.
85. Quoted in Omasombo and Verhaegem, 'Acteur politique', pp. 93–4.
86. François Lumumba, interview (Kinshasa), 20 November 2006.
87. Gibbs, *Political Economy of Third World Intervention*, p. 60.
88. Quoted in Mulopo, *P. Lumumba: Justice pour le héros*, p. 69.
89. Quoted in Omasombo and Verhaegem, 'Acteur politique', p. 109.
90. Quoted in P Halen and J Riesz (eds), 'Un témoignage' in *Patrice Lumumba entre dieu et diable: un héro africain dans ses images* (Paris: l'Harmattan, 1997), p. 93.
91. Quoted in Halen and Riesz (eds), 'Un témoignage', p. 93.
92. Quoted in McKown, *Lumumba: a biography*, p. 61.
93. J van Lierde (ed), *La pensée politique de Patrice Lumumba* (Paris: Présence Africaine, 1963), p. 11.
94. Ludo de Witte, interview (Brussels), 19 July 2006.
95. P Lumumba, *Congo, my country*, p. 173.
96. Van Lierde, *La pensée politique de Patrice Lumumba*, p. 20.
97. Quoted in Omasombo and Verhaegem, 'Acteur politique', p. 175.
98. Mckown, *Lumumba: a biography*, p. 64.
99. Lumumba, *Congo, my country*, p. 142.
100. Ludo de Witte, interview (Brussels), 19 June 2006.
101. H F Weiss, *Political Protest in the Congo*: *The Parti Solidaire Africain During the Independence Struggle* (Princeton: Princeton University Press, 1967), pp. 61, 84.
102. E Simons, R Boyhossian and B Verhaegem, 'Stanleyville 1959: le proces de Patrice Lumumba et les emertes d'octobre', *Cahiers Africains* 17–18 (1995), p. 26.
103. C Legum, *Congo disaster* (London: Penguin, 1961), p. 60.

104. Lumumba, *Congo, my country*, p. 176.
105. Matthias Kemishanga, interview (Kinshasa), 19 November 2006.
106. Matthias Kemishanga, interview (Kinshasa), 19 November 2006.
107. Tony Busselen, interview (Kinshasa), 18 November 2006.
108. P Lumumba, *Congo, my country*, p. 147.
109. Simons, Boyhossian and Verhaegem, 'Stanleyville 1959', p. 131.
110. Van Lierde, *La pensée politique de Patrice Lumumba*, p. 45.
111. Weiss, *Political Protest in the Congo*, pp. 183–5.
112. Lumumba, *Congo, my country*, pp. 136, 141.
113. Van Lierde, *La pensée politique de Patrice Lumumba*, p. 247.
114. F Fanon, *The Wretched of the Earth* (London: Harmondsworth; Penguin, 1967), p. 174.
115. J Molyneux, *What is the Real Marxist Tradition?* (London: Bookmarks, 1985), p. 63.
116. Fanon, *The Wretched of the Earth*, p. 77.
117. Van Lierde, *La pensée politique de Patrice Lumumba*, pp. 100–1.
118. Tony Busselen, interview (Kinshasa), 18 November 2006.
119. Quoted in Omasombo and Verhaegem, 'Acteur politique', pp. 284–5.
120. Van Lierde, *La pensée politique de Patrice Lumumba*, p. 138.
121. Quoted in Mckown, *Lumumba: a biography*, p. 78.
122. Legum, *Congo disaster*, p. 99.
123. Van Lierde, *La pensée politique de Patrice Lumumba*, p. 142.
124. Quoted in Lumumba, *Congo, my country*, p. xiii.
125. Weiss, *Political Protest in the Congo*, p. 37.
126. Panaf Great Lives *Patrice Lumumba*, p. 116.
127. Legum, *Congo disaster*, p. 92.
128. Juliana Lumumba, interview (Kinshasa), 18 November 2006.

129. François Lumumba, interview (Kinshasa), 20 November 2006.
130. Ludo de Witte, interview (Brussels), 19 June 2006.
131. Quoted in Omasombo and Verhaegem, 'Acteur politique', p. 372.
132. *Guardian*, 1 July 1960.
133. Juliana Lumumba, interview (Kinshasa), 18 November 2006.
134. Hochschild, *King Léopold's Ghost*, p. 301,
135. Van Lierde (ed), *Lumumba speaks: The speeches and writings of Patrice Lumumba 1958–1961* (Boston: Little, Brown and Company, 1972), pp. 220–1.
136. Quoted in J C Willame, 'Du portrait au personage. La diabolisation symbolique de Patrice Lumumba dans La Libre Belgique' in Halen and Riesz (eds), *Patrice Lumumba entre dieu et diable*, p. 193.
137. A M Babu, *The Future that works* (Trenton: Africa World Press, 2002), p. 66.
138. Asse Lilombo, interview (Kinshasa), 20 November 2006.
139. Mbara Emmanual 'Emery' Bastin, interview (Kinshasa), 20 November 2006.
140. *La Releve*, 27 August 1960.
141. Ludo de Witte, *The Assassination of Lumumba* (London: Verso, 2001), p. 31, hereafter Ludo de Witte, *Asassination*.
142. Quoted in Mckown, *Lumumba: a biography*, p.111.
143. R Govender, *The Martyrdom of Patrice Lumumba* (London: Neillgo, 1971), pp. 66–7, hereafter Govender, *Martyrdom*.
144. Quoted in Mckown, *Lumumba: a biography*, p. 120.
145. Ludo de Witte, *Assassination*, p. 37.
146. S Simon, 'The Belgian General Strike', *Revolutionary History* 7/1 (1998), pp. 80–133.
147. Ludo de Witte, interview (Brussels), 19 June 2006.
148. Van Lierde (ed), *Lumumba speaks*, p. 293.

149. *Daily Telegraph*, 27 July 1960.
150. Govender, *Martyrdom*, p. 86.
151. J Woddis, *Africa: The Lion Awakes* (London: Lawrence and Wishart, 1961), p. 136.
152. Quoted in Mckown, *Lumumba: a biography*, p. 145.
153. Wrong, *In the Footsteps of Mr Kurtz*, p. 66.
154. Govender, *Martyrdom*, pp. 173–4.
155. S Pisani, *Lumumba Lost* (Xlibris Corporation: 2003), p. 115.
156. Ludo de Witte, *Assassination*, pp. 52–4.
157. Matthais Kemishanga, interview (Kinshasa), 19 November 2006.
158. Van Lierde (ed), *Lumumba speaks*, pp. 421–2.
159. François Lumumba, interview (Kinshasa), 20 November 2006.
160. The conclusions of the report are available online at www.lachambre.be/kvvcr/pdf_sections/comm/lmb/conclusions.pdf.
161. Quoted in Lumumba, *Congo, my country*, p. x.
162. Babu, *The Future*, pp. 195–6.
163. B Berkeley, *The Graves are not yet full: Race, Tribe and Power in the Heart of Africa* (New York: new Republic, 2001), p. 110.
164. Interview, Larry Devlin, BBC Radio 4, 3 March 2007
165. Govender, *Martyrdom*, p. 131.
166. Hochschild, *King Léopold's Ghost*, p. 302.
167. Interview, Larry Devlin, BBC Radio 4, 3 March 2007.
168. See D Lea, Letters, *London Review of Books* http://www.lrb.co.uk/v35/n07/letters#letter5 11 April 2013.
169. See Foreign Office Minutes, FO 371/146650, P Murphy (ed) *British Documents on End of Empire* (London: The Stationary Office, 2005), Series B, Volume 9, pp. 167–9.
170. Van Lierde (ed), *Lumumba speaks*, pp. 421–2.
171. Quoted in Lumumba, *Congo, my country*, p. xvi.

172. Quoted in Panaf Great Lives, *Patrice Lumumba*, p. 163.
173. Ludo de Witte, interview (Brussels), 19 June 2006.
174. Govender, *Martyrdom*, pp. 8–9.
175. Quoted in Patrice Lumumba, *Congo, my country*, p. xxvi.
176. Ludo de Witte, *Assassination*, pp. 151–2.
177. *La Libre Belgique* 'La Mort de Lumumba: cruel et sanglant', 14 February 1961.
178. François Lumumba, interview (Kinshasa), 20 November 2006.
179. Juliana Lumumba, interview (Kinshasa) 18 November, 2006.
180. R Segal, *African Profiles* (London: Penguin, 1963), pp. 184–5.
181. Hochschild, *King Leopold's Ghost*, p. 302.
182. Quoted in Mckown, *Lumumba: a biography*, p.191.
183. François Lumumba, interview (Kinshasa), 20 November 2006.
184. François Lumumba, interview (Kinshasa), 20 November 2006.
185. Juliana Lumumba, interview (Kinshasa), 18 November 2006.
186. François Lumumba, interview (Kinshasa), 20 November 2006.
187. See 'Lumumba's murder to be probed' in *Cape Times*, 14 December, 2012.
188. Van Lierde, *La pensée politique de Patrice Lumumba*, pp. xx–xxi.
189. Van Lierde, *La pensée politique de Patrice Lumumba*, p. xli.
190. Van Lierde, *La pensée politique de Patrice Lumumba*, p. xxxiii.
191. Van Lierde, *La pensée politique de Patrice Lumumba*, p. xlii.
192. F. Fanon *Pour la révolution africaine* (Paris: La Dévouverte, 2001), p. 219.
193. Ludo de Witte, interview (Brussels), 19 June 2006.

194. Quoted in Lumumba, *Congo, my country*, p. xxix.
195. See L Devlin's recent memoir *Chief of Station, Congo: Fighting the Cold War in a Hot Zone* (New York: Public Affairs Books, 2007).
196. François Lumumba, interview (Kinshasa), 20 November 2006.

Year	Age	Life
1925		2 July: Born in the village of Onalua, in the territory of Katako-Kombe in the Kasai Province.
1944	19	Travels to Stanleyville.

Year	History	Culture
1925	Christiania, the Norwegian capital, is renamed Oslo. In Italy, Mussolini announces that he will take dictatorial powers. Paul von Hindenburg, former military leader, is elected President of Germany. Hitler reorganises Nazi Party. Locarno conference discusses the question of a security pact. Locarno Treaty later signed in London.	Thomas Mofolo's *Chaka the Zulu* is written in the South African language of Sotho. Noel Coward, *Hay Fever.* Franz Kafka, *The Trial.* Virginia Woolf, *Mrs Dalloway.* Pablo Picasso, *Three Dancers.* Marc Chagall, *The Drinking Green Pig.* Lyonel Feininger, *Tower.* Alban Berg, *Wozzek.* Ferruccio Busconi, *Doctor Faust.* Film: *Battleship Potemkin.*
1944	Free French politicians and high-ranking representatives from the French African colonies met in Brazzaville (today's Republic of the Congo). The Brazzaville Conference recommends political reforms for France's colonies.	Carl Jung, *Psychology and Religion.* Michael Tippett, *A Child of Our Time.* T S Eliot, *Four Quartets.* Terrence Rattigan, *The Winslow Boy.* Tennessee Williams, *The Glass Menagerie.* Film: *Double Indemnity. Henry V. Meet Me in St Louis.*

Year	Age	Life
1947	22	Studies at the Post Office School of Léopoldville.
1951	25	Marries Pauline Opango.

Year	History	Culture
1947	Hungary is reassigned its 1938 frontiers. The Moscow Conference fails over the problem of Germany. 'Truman Doctrine' pledges to support 'free peoples resisting subjugation by armed minorities or outside pressures'. US Secretary of State calls for relief aid to Europe. Indonesian independence movement rises against Dutch troops.	The journal *Presence Africaine* is established, promoting an African perspective on the world. Edinburgh Festival is founded. Albert Camus, *The Plague*. Anne Frank, *The Diary of Anne Frank*. Tennessee Williams, *A Streetcar Named Desire*. Le Corbusier, Unité d'Habitation Marseille, France. Films: *Monsieur Verdoux*. *Black Narcissus*.
1951	French elections cause ministerial crisis; Pleven forms coalition of the Centre. Peace Treaty with Japan is signed by 49 powers, though not by USSR. Peron is re-elected president of Argentina. Chichekli leads Syrian coup. Libya becomes independent federation. Electric power is produced from atomic energy in USA.	Shaaban Robert of Tanganyika (today's Tanzania) publishes his best-known work *Kusadikika* which explores political developments in colony. Henry Moore, *Reclining Figure*. Benjamin Britten, *Billy Budd*. Stravinsky, *The Rake's Progress*. Isaac Asimov, *Foundation*. J D Salinger, *The Catcher in the Rye*. Herman Wouk, *The Caine Mutiny*. Jean-Paul Sartre, *Le Diable et le Bon Dieux*. Film: *A Streetcar Named Desire*. *The African Queen*. *The Man in the White Suit*.

Year	Age	Life
1954	29	5 February: Recorded in the 'Register of the civilised indigenous population'. 5 March: Elected president of the *Association des Évolués de Stanleyville*; Lumumba is president or secretary of seven associations in the city.
1956	31	Travels to Belgium on a government-sponsored tour. 6 July Imprisoned for embezzlement. Writes his book *The Congo land of the future is it threatened?* in prison.

Year	History	Culture
1954	Yugoslav National Assembly adopts new constitution. Tito is elected first president of Yugoslav Republic. European Political Community constitution is drafted and later adopted. Joseph Stalin dies. In USSR, Nikita Khrushchev is appointed first secretary of central committee of Communist Party. Konrad Adenauer forms new government in West Germany.	Britten, *The Turn of the Screw*. Kingsley Amis, *Lucky Jim*. William Golding, *Lord of the Flies*. J R R Tolkein, *The Lord of the Rings I, II*. (*III* in 1955) Tennessee Williams, *Cat on a Hot Tin Roof*. Films: *On the Waterfront*. *Rear Window*. *The Seven Samurai*.
1956	President Nasser emerges victorious after the Suez Crisis, forcing French and British troops to withdraw. New government, including non-communists is formed in Hungary. It renounces the Warsaw Treaty. Soviet forces attack Budapest. Fidel Castro lands in Cuba and begins guerrilla warfare to overthrow Batista's government.	Karl Mannheim, *Essays on the Sociology of Culture*. First computer-programming language is invented in USA. A J Ayer, *The Problem of Knowledge*. Britten, *The Prince of the Pagodas*. Lerner/Lowe, *My Fair Lady*. Rock'n'Roll dominates the dance floors. John Osborne, *Look Back in Anger*. Films: *Baby Doll*. *The King and I*. *A Town Like Alice*.

Year	Age	Life
1957	32	7 September: Released from prison; starts working in the Bracongo Brewery in Léopoldville the following day.
1958	33	10 October: Elected president of the *Mouvement National Congolais*. Attends the Sixth Pan-African Conference in Ghana.

Year	History	Culture
1957	Ghana becomes first independent black state in Africa under Kwame Nkrumah Belgium, France, West Germany, Italy, Luxembourg and Netherlands sign Treaty of Rome establishing the European Economic Community (EEC). USA, Britain, France and West Germany issue declaration on principles of German reunification and call for free elections. Sweeping victory for Konrad Adenauer in West German elections.	Kenneth Clark, *The Nude.* Jack Kerouac, *On the Road.* Patrick White, *Voss.* Samuel Beckett, *Endgame.* Bernstein, *West Side Story.* Poulenc, *Les Dialogues des Carmelites* (opera). Francis Bacon, *Screaming Nurse.* Le Corbusier, Tokyo Museum. Films: *The Bridge on the River Kwai. The Prince and the Showgirl.*
1958	Egypt and Syria form United Arab Republic. De Gaulle becomes President of France. USSR grants loan to Nasser for building Aswan Dam. Prince Charles created Prince of Wales.	Wittgenstein, *The Blue Book. The Brown Book* (posthumous). Iris Murdoch, *The Bell.* Boris Pasternak, *Dr Zhivago.* Harold Pinter, *The Birthday Party.* Johnson and van der Rohe, Seagram Building New York. Mark Rothko, *Seagram Murals.* Benjamin Britten, *Noye's Fludde.* Perry Como, *Magic Moments.* Films: *Gigi. Touch of Evil. Vertigo.*

Year	Age	Life
1959	34	4 January: Rebellion in Léopoldville, hundreds killed. ABAKO proscribed; Lumumba starts to build the MNC. Belgium's de-colonisation proposals announced in the *'Declaration Gouvernementale'* explain that independence will come 'gradually'
		1 November: Lumumba arrested in Stanleyville for inciting a riot.
1960	35	20 January: Round Table Conference opens in Brussels, Lumumba released from prison to attend.
		11–25 May: Elections held in the Congo, victory for Lumumba's MNC.
		10 May: *Loi Fondamentale* (Basic law) on structure of the future Congolese state is passed by the Belgian senate.
		29 June: Belgian-Congolese Treaty of Friendship signed.
		30 June: Independence declared; Lumumba makes a speech condemning colonialism.
		5 July: First mutiny of soldiers in the *Force Publique*.
		11 July: Tshombe announces the Independent State of Katanga.
		22 July: UN Security Council calls on Belgian troops to withdraw from the Congo.
		2–8 August: Lumumba visits a number of African states to gather support.
		25–30 August: Conference of Independent African States held in Léopoldville.

Year	History	Culture
1959	Liu Shaoqi elected chairman of Chinese Republic in succession to Mao Zedong. UN votes against admission of People's Republic of China. UN General Assembly condemns apartheid in South Africa and all other racial discrimination. Conference in Stockholm, Finance ministers of Austria, Denmark, Britain, Norway, Portugal, Sweden and Switzerland establish European Free Trade Association. Britain and Arab Republic (Syria and Egypt) resume diplomatic relations.	Saul Bellow, *Henderson the Rain King.* Günther Grass, *The Tin Drum.* Brendan Behan, *The Hostage.* Harold Pinter, *The Caretaker.* Frank Lloyd Wright, Beth Shalom Synagogue, Pennsylvania. Francis Poulenc, *La voix humaine* (opera). Rodgers/Hammerstein, *The Sound of Music.* Motown Records founded in Detroit, USA. Films: *Ben Hur. Some Like it Hot. North by Northwest.*
1960	Sharpeville Massacre in South Africa: during a demonstration police panic and kill 69, injure 186. Following strikes, demonstrations and marches, state of emergency is proclaimed in South Africa. European Free Trade Association comes into force. Brezhnev replaces Voroshilov as President of USSR. Democrat John F Kennedy wins US presidential election. OECD treaty signed in Paris by USA, Canada and 18 member countries of OEEC.	AJ Ayer, *Logical Positivism.* John Updike, *Rabbit Run.* Alain Robbe-Grillet, *Dans la labyrinthe.* Robert Bolt, *A Man for All Seasons.* Frank Lloyd Wright, Guggenheim Museum, New York. Benjamin Britten, *A Midsummer Night's Dream.* Lionel Bart, *Oliver!* Films: *The Magnificent Seven. Psycho. Saturday Night and Sunday Morning.*

Year	Age	Life
1961	35	17 January: Lumumba, Maurice Mpolo and Joseph Okito transferred to Katanga; late evening the three men are beaten and murdered. 13 February: Katangan Minister of the Interior Godefroid Munungo announces the news of the death of the prisoners.

Year	History	Culture
1961	USA severs diplomatic relations with Cuba. Prime Minister Verwoerd announces that South Africa will leave the British Commonwealth on 31 May. Khrushchev proposes German peace conference to President Kennedy. USA and USSR begin disarmament talks in Washington DC. Construction of the Berlin Wall.	Frantz Fanon writes his influential book *The Wretched of the Earth*. The author dies the same year Jean Anouilh, *Becket*. John Osborne, *Luther*. In London, Hardwick's neo-classical arch at Euston Station is demolished. Henry Mancini, *Moon River*. Elvis Presley, *Are you lonesome tonight?* The Rolling Stones form. The Beatles debut in Liverpool. Films: *Breakfast at Tiffany's*. *West Side Story*. *Victim*.

Sources and acknowledgements

This biography of Patrice Lumumba has drawn on other studies of his life, notably two extraordinary volumes written by Jean Omasombo and Benoit Verhaegem. Both have appeared as special issues in the French language journal *Cahiers Africains*. The first study, *Patrice Lumumba: Jeunesse et apprentissage politique 1925–1956* focuses on Patrice Lumumba's childhood and life in Stanleyville. The second volume, *Acteur politique: de la prison aux portes du pouvoir*, describes his life from prison to independence. Together these studies are an extremely thorough examination of Lumumba's pre-independence life. They presents the biographer with an incredibly detailed account of Lumumba's life – often through the words of his contemporaries – and much which has never before been published. Neither of these volumes is available in English.

Many of the best-known books focus on the last period of Lumumba's life, such as Ludo de Witte's *The Assassination of Lumumba*, which caused a parliamentary scandal in Belgium. Ludo de Witte's book is a superb expose of the role of the Belgian state in Lumumba's murder. Other studies include biographies written in the 1960s and 1970s, and many are out of print and in French. This means that there is very little on Lumumba's entire life for an English speaking audience. Robin Mckown's *Lumumba, a biography* was notable in the period (it was published in 1969), for being very sympathetic to Lumumba. Another other much cited biography is Pierre de Vos's *Vie et mort de Lumumba*, published in 1961. There is also the important new biography by George Nzongola-Ntalaja; *Patrice Lumumba*, published in 2014.

By far the best source of Lumumba's own writing is *Lumumba speaks: The speeches and writings of Patrice Lumumba 1958–1961* edited by his collaborator and comrade Jean van Lierde. This collection is a translation from the French edition that appeared in 1963. This is a superb collection of Lumumba's speeches and interviews was published with a critical introduction by Jean-Paul Sartre. Lumumba's only book came out the year that he was assassinated, and in contentious circumstances. In English it was published in 1962 under the title *Congo, my country*. This is a fascinating insight into Lumumba's ideas in 1956. For this book I have used my own translations from French, and where necessary I have alternated between French and English editions of the same work.

I have also drawn extensively on interviews with members of Lumumba's family, comrades and sympathisers. Juliana Lumumba was extremely helpful answering my sometimes impertinent questions during an interview in Kinshasa in November 2006, and also patient with my endless stream of telephone queries. François Lumumba, who now leads his father's political party the MNC-L, agreed to an interview at very short notice. Asse Lilombo and Mbara Emmanual 'Emery' Bastin, both militants in the MNC-L, gave fascinating personal accounts of independence in the Congo. Matthias Kemishanga was one of Lumumba's most loyal comrades and a Member of Parliament in the country's first elections. Kemishanga was with Lumumba when Mobutu's police caught up with them as they tried to escape to Stanleyville in November 1960. He described the hopes of independence, and the pride he felt at having always honoured his pledge to remain loyal to the MNC and Lumumba.

I also received generous support from Ludo de Witte, who read and commented on an earlier version of the book. His encyclopedic knowledge of the Congo, Lumumba and Belgian politics was invaluable on numerous occasions. Ludo de Witte was also interviewed for the book. Tony Busselen and Ludo Martens, both experts on Lumumba and the Congo, were generous with their time, contacts and knowledge. Andy Wynne and David Renton have both read and commented on early drafts of the book. Peter Alexander's typically penetrating remarks were extremely useful.

This new edition has been greatly assisted by Haus who has enthusiastically promoted the biography. I have also recently edited a collection of Lumumba's writings, *Voices of Liberation: Lumumba* (Cape Town, HSRC: 2014), which has allowed me to return to the events of Lumumba's short life. I am grateful to the Institute of Commonwealth Studies at the University of London and particularly to Philip Murphy for continuing to provide me with a research home.

Leo Zeilig
September, 2014

Selected further reading in English

Unfortunately there are few books on the life on Patrice Lumumba in English still in print.

Other biographies

Robin Mckown's *Lumumba, a biography* (New York: Doubleday, 1969) is long out of print but can be bought on the internet. But the 'authorless' *Patrice Lumumba* (London: Panaf, 1973) was reprinted in 2002 as part of the Panaf Great Lives series. These are valuable sources, but both are dated. Mckown's book has a slightly patronising tone towards the Congolese, and the Panaf book is overloaded with occasionally tiresome political rhetoric. By far the best source on Lumumba's assassination is Ludo de Witte's brilliant *The Assassination of Lumumba* (London: Verso, 2001).

Works by Lumumba

Lumumba's own work *Congo, my country* (New York: Frederick A. Praeger, 1962) can be found in bookshops and online. Jean van Lierde (ed), *Lumumba speaks: The speeches and writings of Patrice Lumumba 1958–1961* (Boston: Little, Brown and Company, 1972) is a superb collection, with a fascinating introduction by Jean-Paul Sartre.

Colonial history

One of the best books to have appeared recently is Adam

Hochschild's *King Léopold's Ghost: A Story of Greed, Terror and Heroism in Colonial Africa* (London: Pan Books, 1998).

Recent history

George Nzongola-Ntalaja, *The Congo from Leopold to Kabila: A people's History* (London: Zed Books, 2002) is a splendid introduction to the recent history of the Congo. Another book, that presents a radical background to the country's history is *The Congo: Plunder and Resistance* (London: Zed Books, 2006) by David Renton, David Seddon and Leo Zeilig.

Decolonisation and class

Franz Fanon's *The Wretched of the Earth* (London: Penguin, 1967) unpicks the nature of national liberation and the question of class during the decolonisation of Africa. Tony Cliff's pamphlet 'Deflected Permanent Revolution' in *International Socialism* 1 (1963) on the role of the intelligentsia is an indispensable guide to understanding the character of the class struggle in the Third World during the period of anti-colonialism. Both of these texts are available online.

Academic texts

An excellent academic text on the Congo is Theodore Trefon, Saskia Van Hoyweghen and Stephan Smis's edited collection of essay's and studies on 'State Failure in the Congo: Perceptions and Realities' in the *Review of African Political Economy* 93/4 (2002). Even if some of the contributions are quite hard going there is lots of useful information.

Picture sources

The author and publishers wish to express their thanks to the following sources of illustrative material and/or permission to reproduce it. They will make proper acknowledgements in future editions in the event that any omissions have occurred.

Getty Images: pp. i, ii, 37, 75, 101, 110, 118, 132, 134; *Horizon*. The magazine of the Rhodesian Selection Trust group of companies. March 1962. Courtesy John Edmonds: pp. 23, 33, 64, 65, 84, 92, 139, 140; Topham Picturepoint: pp. 2, 5, 9, 11, 15, 50, 105, 112, 118, 121, 125, 138; Leo Zeilig: p. 147

Index

NB All family relationships are to Patrice Lumumba, unless otherwise stated.

X